Caring for Digital Data in Archaeology:

A Guide to Good Practice

Archaeology Data Service and Digital Antiquity

Oxbow Books
Oxford and Oakville

Produced by Oxbow Books on behalf of the Archaeology Data Service
and the Center for Digital Antiquity

ISBN 978-1-78297-249-5
ISSN 1463-5194

A CIP record for this book is available from the British Library 2013

This book is available direct from

Oxbow Books, Oxford, UK

(Phone: 01865-214249; Fax 01865-794449)

and

The David Brown Book Company

PO Box 511, Oakville, CT 06779, USA

(Phone: 860-945-9329; Fax 860-945-9468)

or from our website

www.oxbowbooks.com

Library of Congress Cataloging-in-Publication Data

Caring for digital data in archaeology : a guide to good practice.
pages cm. -- (Archaeology Data Service and Digital Antiquity guides to good practice, ISSN 1463-5194)
Edited by Adam Brin, Center for Digital Antiquity, Francis P. McManamon, Center for Digital Antiquity and Kieron Niven, Archaeology Data Service.
Includes bibliographical references.
ISBN 978-1-78297-249-5
1. Archaeology--Computer network resources--Handbooks, manuals, etc. 2. Archival materials--Digitization--Handbooks, manuals, etc. 3. Archaeology--Data processing--Handbooks, manuals, etc. 4. Archaeology--Methodology--Handbooks, manuals, etc. 5. Digital libraries--Management--Handbooks, manuals, etc. 6. Digital preservation--Handbooks, manuals, etc. I. Brin, Adam. II. McManamon, Francis P. III. Niven, Kieron. IV. Archaeology Data Service. V. Digital Antiquity.

CC82.9.C37 2013
025.8'4--dc23

2013012993

Contents

Figures

Tables

ACKNOWLEDGEMENTS

This publication has been created as an extension to a two-year project to revise and extend the online *Guides to Good Practice.* The project has been jointly undertaken by the UK Archaeology Data Service and the US Center for Digital Antiquity and funded by the Andrew W. Mellon Foundation.

As with the online *Guides*, this publication incorporates, revises and summarizes extensive material from a number of previous Archaeology Data Service publications:

Archaeology Data Service (2008) *VENUS Preservation Handbook.*

Austin, T. and Mitcham, J. (2007) *Preservation and Management Strategies for Exceptionally Large Data Formats: 'Big Data'.* Archaeology Data Service.

Austin, T., Bateman, J., Jeffrey, S., Mitcham, J. and Niven, K. (2009) *Marine Remote Sensing and Photogrammetry: A Guide to Good Practice.* Archaeology Data Service.

Richards, J. and Robinson, D. (eds) (2000) *Digital Archives from Excavation and Fieldwork: Guide to Good Practice.* Second Edition. AHDS Guides to Good Practice.

The authors and editors of this publication would like to acknowledge and thank those involved in these previous guides for allowing their work to form such a major contribution to this publication.

This Guide was edited by:

Adam Brin, Center for Digital Antiquity
Francis P. McManamon, Center for Digital Antiquity
Kieron Niven, Archaeology Data Service

The editors of this Guide would also like to extend their thanks to all those who have worked so hard to bring it to publication, including:

Tim Evans, Archaeology Data Service
Catherine Hardman, Archaeology Data Service
Val Kinsler, 100% Proof
Julian Richards, Archaeology Data Service

At the Center for Digital Antiquity our work on this publication and overall on the *Guides* project was assisted by:

Russell Alleen-Willems, Center for Digital Antiquity
Kirsten Clary, Center for Digital Antiquity
James deVos, Center for Digital Antiquity
Leigh Anne Ellison, Center for Digital Antiquity
Keith Kintigh, Center for Digital Antiquity
Shelby Manney, Center for Digital Antiquity
Scott Thompson, Center for Digital Antiquity
Josh Watts, Center for Digital Antiquity
Mary Whelan, Arizona State University Libraries

Part 1. Digital Archiving: An Introduction to this Guide

1.1 ABOUT THESE GUIDELINES

Modern archaeological projects have the capacity to create large quantities of digital information, whether from the on-site recording of excavation and survey data, specialized data sets developed during pre- and post-excavation analysis, or publication of interpretative maps and plans. Digital information is created at every stage of a project, from fieldwork to assessment, analysis, reporting, and dissemination. Within the discipline, there has been an increasing awareness that data, not just artifacts and paper records, are part of the primary collection and should be preserved and archived. The current trend of moving away from physical and toward digital recording of information has made the lack of preservation of digital data an even larger problem. In many cases, digital data may be the only product of a project, and without digital preservation, all records will be lost. The primary aim of this guide, along with the online *Guides to Good Practice*, is to provide information on the best way to create, manage, and document digital data produced during the course of an archaeological project. This guide aims to improve the practice of depositing and preserving digital information safely within an archive for future use.

A fundamental principle of this publication is that digital data produced from archaeological investigation should be managed and archived in a digital format so that it can be accessed, used, and preserved. This approach eliminates the need for costly re-digitization in the future while ensuring maximum accessibility and reusability of the data. Digital archiving also preserves the functionality of data sets in applications such as Access or Excel, or contained within Geographic Information Systems (GIS), Computer Aided Design (CAD), and relational databases that simply could not exist outside of a digital medium.

1.1.1 History of the Guides to Good Practice

This publication forms part of ongoing work aimed at revising and expanding upon an original series of *Guides to Good Practice* created by the Archaeology Data Service (ADS) as part of the UK's Arts and Humanities Data Service (AHDS). Between 1998 and 2002, six *Guides* were published covering the creation and archiving of archaeological data within a number of key project types including aerial photography, excavation and geophysical survey, GIS, CAD, and virtual reality. The original series of *Guides* individually drew together a number of key authors and contributors, all active in their respective fields, in order to produce widely relevant material that was subsequently reviewed, accepted, and utilized in academic and non-academic circles.

The Online *Guides to Good Practice*

In 2009 a new project was launched to broaden and update the original *Guides to Good Practice*. This project was carried out by the Archaeology Data Service, in the UK, and the Center for Digital Antiquity (Digital Antiquity), a US-based organization devoted to enhancing preservation of and access to digital records of archaeological investigations (Center for Digital Antiquity 2012; Kintigh and Altschul 2010; McManamon and Kintigh 2010; McManamon et al. 2010). The project resulted in the creation of an updated and integrated set of online *Guides to Good Practice* that combined the original independent publications and expanded into previously uncovered areas (http://guidestogoodpractice.org).

The aim of the updated version of the online *Guides* is to identify and describe key considerations in digital archiving, for example, documentation, file formats, metadata creation, and data migration. Although much of the content in the original ADS *Guides* remains applicable, in many areas the relevant technologies have developed considerably over the subsequent years. These changes have spawned new approaches and formats, as well as requiring different or further documentation in order to understand and reuse the data. In addition, many existing areas of data production have now fallen into the digital realm with 'born-digital' reports, images and video files becoming commonplace components of many archaeological projects. The online *Guides* aim to address these developments, and provide concise guidance on managing and archiving the wide array of digital objects that are now core components of modern archaeological research.

The online *Guides* also aim to provide the basis for archaeological project workflows to create digital data that can be archived effectively both by Digital Antiquity's the Digital Archaeological Record (tDAR) in the US, and by the ADS in the UK. The development of the online *Guides* has involved close collaboration between the ADS and teams in the US at the University of Arkansas and at Arizona State University. As a result of this collaboration, where the original *Guides to Good Practice* were written primarily to address archaeological practice in the UK, the online *Guides* provide guidance that is more widely relevant. The scope includes the UK and Europe, but also the United States, North and South America, and other parts of the world.

About the Print Edition

This publication – *Caring for Digital Data in Archaeology* – distils the general, introductory sections of the online *Guides* to summarize the key concepts and requirements of digital archiving for a wide archaeological audience. This guide specifically addresses the concept and process of digital archiving, how this can be applied to the lifecycle of archaeological data, and how to deal with documents, data sets, and images that are common products of archaeological projects.

1.2 HOW TO USE THIS GUIDE - AUDIENCE, PURPOSE, AND USE

The goal of this guide is to inform and educate archaeologists, project and program managers, and other interested parties, about important concepts, techniques and aspects of digital preservation.

Users of this publication will find some sections written for a general audience and others that include more technical information. We have included some of the technical information so that general readers, who will include program and project managers who must plan for digital curation of archaeological project results, can get a sense of the level of technical detail that proper digital archiving for documents, data sets, images, and other kinds of files requires. For those technical experts who use this publication the more general sections will give them an overview of the objectives to which their particular skills contribute.

When and how to use this guide

- During the planning phase of a project to identify relevant issues.
- Throughout the project as a reference on specific issues.
- Ahead of the deposit of files in a digital archive or repository.

1.2.1 Intended Audience

A wide variety of organizations are both creating and retaining digital data from archaeological projects – illustrated by the results of *Strategies for Digital Data* (Condron et al. 1999: 29–32), the ADS 'Big Data' project (Austin and Mitcham 2007) and a more recent survey of archaeological repositories in the US by Digital Antiquity (Watts 2011). While current methods for preservation and access to data vary widely, nearly all of these organizations agree that careful management of digital archaeological resources is an important aspect of responsible archaeological stewardship.

For this reason both this guide, and the online *Guides to Good Practice,* are aimed at the following audiences:

- **Federal, state, and tribal agencies that manage archaeological resources on the land they administer**, e.g., the Bureau of Land Management, Department of Defense services, the Forest Service and the National Park Service.

- **Agencies that fund, or require as part of permit applications, archaeological investigations** that result in collections and associated records, e.g., the Federal Highway Administration and the Federal Energy Regulatory Commission in the United States and national heritage agencies and local authorities in the UK.
- **State and Tribal Historic Preservation Offices** that manage information about archaeological resources within their state or reservation jurisdictions.
- **Museum and university researchers** who undertake archaeological research and produce digital data as part of their activities.
- **Cultural Resource Management (CRM) firms** that carry out archaeological studies under contracts or cooperative agreements with public agencies or private organizations and produce archaeological data as part of their investigations.
- **Museums and other national or regional repositories** that are responsible for ensuring access to and long-term preservation of archaeological collections and associated records.
- **National and local voluntary groups and societies**.

The audiences outlined above can, in the broadest sense, be divided into two main groups: (i) those funding and creating data and (ii) those caring for or curating the digital data after its creation. In many cases both of these roles may be undertaken within the same organization, either by the same individuals or by separate departments. The following points aim to outline how both groups can best use these guides.

Data Creators and Funders

- Raise awareness of best practices, standards, and common workflows.
- Provide guidance on:
    - Evaluating and selecting digital archives.
    - Successful workflow strategies that are conducive to digital archiving.
    - Appropriate project and workflow documentation.
- Assist in short, mid-term, and long-term planning:
    - Identifying issues not traditionally considered within the context of archiving that are critical to future preservation and use.
- Inform creators about copyright, access and ethical obligations that should be considered throughout the process.

Data Curators

- Raise awareness of best practices, standards, and common workflows.
- Provide guidance on issues and file formats specific to archaeology.
- Ensure access.
- Assist in short, mid-term, and long-term planning.
- Identify issues around copyright, access and ethical obligations that should be considered.
- Ensure that digital archives follow the principles related to access and preservation established for 'trusted digital repositories' (e.g. the ISO 16363 Standard for Trusted Digital Repositories; Center for Research Libraries 2007, RLG 2002).

1.2.2 Using this Guide

The online *Guides to Good Practice*, together with this guide, have been created to allow flexibility in how they are used. General preservation topics are discussed in Part 1 of this guide within the context of archaeological investigations, research, and resource management, with an overview of digital archiving practice and guidance. This section addresses the fundamentals of digital preservation and general archival strategies.

Following this, Part 2 looks at common project lifecycle elements. This section covers general broad themes that should be considered at the outset of a project, such as potential data sources, file-name conventions, metadata creation and documentation formats, specifications and copyright considerations.

Part 3 looks at selected techniques and file-type specific issues, together with archive structuring and deposit. This section covers common file types that are frequently created by archaeological projects. A range of file types is covered, including documents and texts, databases, spreadsheets, and raster and vector images. The online *Guides* contain a wider range of file types and techniques including digital audio, video, and sensory data. In cases where the online version contains greater detail, links to the relevant online material are included.

The structure of this guide is designed so that users can proceed logically from the introductory material to the specific chapters of interest and then conclude with the 'structuring and depositing' sections. While many of the sections have been written to be used independently, particularly in the online *Guides*, users are advised to be aware of the wider preservation issues raised in the introductory chapters when using the technique or file-type focused sections.

In addition to the basic components chapters covered here in Part 3, the online *Guides* address the preservation of data resulting from common data collection, processing and analysis techniques such as aerial and geophysical survey, laser scanning, GIS and CAD. As with the basic components section, these chapters largely deal with each technique as a workflow in isolation but link, where relevant, to other online sections where certain data can be seen as a discrete input or output.

Getting More Information

This guide summarizes much of the introductory material in the online *Guides to Good Practice*. For more information and advice on material not here, please see the online *Guides* at:

http://www.guidestogoodpractice.org

How to Cite the Guides

This published guide, although linked to the online *Guides to Good Practice*, should be considered as a single publication and cited as:

> Archaeology Data Service and the Center for Digital Antiquity (2013) *Caring for Digital Data in Archaeology: A Guide to Good Practice*. Oxbow Books.

The online *Guides to Good Practice* should also be considered as a single publication encompassing a number of individually authored chapters. The different chapters and sections can be cited as shown in the following examples:

> Archaeology Data Service and the Center for Digital Antiquity (2011) 'About these Guidelines', in Archaeology Data Service and Center for Digital Antiquity *Guides to Good Practice*. Archaeology Data Service, University of York, UK. http://guidestogoodpractice.org/g2gp/GuideAim

> Payne, A. (2011) 'Laser Scanning for Archaeology: A Guide to Good Practice', in Archaeology Data Service and the Center for Digital Antiquity *Guides to Good Practice*. Archaeology Data Service, University of York, UK. http://guidestogoodpractice.org/g2gp/LaserScan_Toc

1.3 WHAT IS DIGITAL ARCHIVING?

Digital archiving is different from traditional archiving. Traditional archiving practice seeks to preserve physical objects (e.g., artifacts, samples, paper, photographs, microfilm) that carry information. Digital archiving preserves the information regardless of the media on which that information is stored. Computer disks and other magnetic and optical media degrade, and the information on them is lost unless it has been moved to other media. Software and hardware change rapidly: the physical media on which digital data are stored are impermanent. Other methods are necessary to ensure wide access to and long-term preservation of digital data.

Archaeology is in a special position with respect to archiving because archaeological fieldwork, which creates archaeological data, also destroys the *in situ* archaeological evidence itself. Increasingly, the digital record may be the only source of information about archaeological research materials, as more materials are 'born-digital'. It is essential, therefore, that the digital records that describe archaeological resources be made accessible and that their preservation be ensured. Providing access and long-term preservation are the goals of digital archiving.

1.3.1 The Goals and Principles of Digital Archiving

The overall goals of digital archiving are simple:

- Ensure the long-term preservation of digital data so that it remains usable in the future.
- Permit easy, wide, and appropriate access to digital data.

The points below present an outline of the key issues to be considered when creating digital materials.

- Ensure that existing digital data are safeguarded and deposited in an appropriate digital archive.
- When choosing a digital archive, ensure that it conforms to existing standards and guidelines on how data should be structured, preserved and accessed.
- All digital materials should ideally be deposited in a digital archiving facility or collections repository where they can be properly accessed, curated, and maintained for the future.
- The key to successful digital archiving is thorough documentation of the data, how they were collected, what standards were used to describe them and how they have been managed since collection.

- If there are concerns that some data (e.g., specific site location information) needs to be kept confidential (as required by the Archaeological Resource Protection Act (ARPA) in the US), a means of easily separating these data from non-confidential data must be developed for reports, analytical data sets, and for displaying site locations on maps. It is also essential that this process is documented and deposited as part of the archive.
- There is generally no need to preserve interim versions of final digital files. Exceptions to this include interim data sets where either data or text is subsequently discarded or edited for final publication. These issues are discussed in Part 2 of this guide.
- When digitizing or scanning from paper records, do not automatically discard the paper originals when complete. Offer them to relevant documentary archives. Digital archiving is not a reason to discard the physical archive, but may increase access or use of the collection.
- Although the digital, paper records, and physical archaeological collections may be separated, proper cross-referencing between physical collections and digital records help ensure the integrity of the complete archive .

It is recommended that the collection or creation of digital data sets be planned at the outset of a project and incorporated into project scopes of work and specifications. It is recognized that funding agencies must acknowledge such requirements if widespread implementation is ever to be achieved. In accordance with the principles presented above, digital archives should at least provide an index to archaeological sites, finds and paper archives and at best provide access to digital records of data, material, documentation, interpretation and analyses.

1.3.2 Case Studies Illustrating the Need for Digital Archiving

Two examples, one from the UK and another from the US, illustrate potential problems when planning for a digital archive is not incorporated as part of project planning and execution.

The Newham Archive: A Case Study of the Loss of Digital Data

This problem has been effectively demonstrated through work to rescue the contents of the Newham Museum Archaeological Service digital archive. The Archaeological Service was closed down in 1998 and, although its physical collections are still curated by the London boroughs of Newham, Redbridge and Waltham Forest, the digital archive was passed to the ADS. The digital archive represented all the work that was digitized during Newham Archaeological Service fieldwork and post-excavation analysis, along with project designs over a period of about ten years. This archive was delivered to the ADS on 230 floppy disks containing over 6000 files. Much of the data was held in archaic formats or in proprietary software and significant time and effort were required to rescue these files. Unfortunately around 10–15% of the files are still inaccessible and the data that they contain are effectively lost. An additional problem was that the archive was inadequately documented and it was often difficult to reconstruct which files belonged to each project. As a result, there are a number of 'orphaned' data sets, including a large cemetery database, which have been rescued but have little reuse potential.

The Newham Museum Archaeological Service digital archive had two main problems:

1. Data held in non-preservation file formats, i.e. proprietary file formats that have gone out of use.
2. Non-existent data or project documentation.

The Newham digital archive is probably typical of the digital information resources of archaeological units. There are many archaeology units with archives of files in redundant formats, without explicit information relating them to sites, containing unexplained coding and in unknown states of completion (cf. Condron et al. 1999). These files may also be stored on unsuitable media in poor physical storage conditions. In short, there may be large amounts of 'archived' archaeological information that can never be accessed again.

The Newham Museum Service digital archive is a depressing and salutary tale. It developed as a working tool to help the Service write up and manage its archaeological projects and, in this respect, the archive was fit for its original purpose. The concept of digital project archiving was still in its infancy when the Newham archive developed. As there were no published strategies or methodologies to ensure the effective preservation of digital data at the time, the poor condition of the Newham archive is understandable.

Soil Systems, Inc.: A Study in Data Recovery

Soil Systems, Inc. (SSI) was a prolific, successful cultural resource management firm that conducted archaeological projects throughout the American Southwest for more than twenty years. Based in Phoenix, AZ, the firm concentrated its work in the state of Arizona and completed a number of very large archaeological compliance projects in the Phoenix metropolitan area. The firm was perhaps most widely known for its extensive and thorough excavations at Pueblo Grande, one of the largest and most influential Hohokam sites in the Phoenix Basin. SSI's work at Pueblo Grande spanned at least five separate testing and/or data recovery projects that took place over the course of more than a decade. The firm's efforts resulted in an impressive set of data that covers most of the known extent of Pueblo Grande. This collection of data and documents alone may rival, in extent and in detail, any other data collection from a single site in the American Southwest.

Unfortunately, SSI closed in 2008, a victim of the worldwide financial crisis that began that year. Most of SSI's physical collections and records (i.e. field notes, paper data records and artifacts) were curated either at the Arizona State Museum, University of Arizona or at Pueblo Grande Museum, Phoenix, AZ. When digital data were created, some of the finalized data tables were converted to text formats and passed to the Arizona State Museum or Pueblo Grande Museum along with physical records and artifact collections. However, the majority of SSI's digital data and records that document the archaeological projects they completed in Arizona, New Mexico, Colorado, Utah, and Nevada, remained in digital database files set up using proprietary formats on local hard drives and servers. In addition, nearly all of the digital data associated with several large projects that SSI was completing at its closure were not passed on to state or municipal repositories.

SSI's digital data for most of its archaeological projects were stored in Advanced Revelations (AREV) version 3.1, an early, MS-DOS based relational database platform. Provenance and artifact analysis data for more than 50 separate projects, including several Pueblo Grande projects, were held in AREV file formats. Spatial data were stored in other formats on SSI's server and on individual, local hard drives. Since SSI produced most of their site maps and report figures in AutoCad, vast quantities of spatial data were stored in now-outdated AutoCad file formats. Finally, individual analyses, integrated data tables, draft reports, and final reports were stored in multiple file formats on the company server.

Thus, at SSI's closure, digital data for at least a hundred archaeological projects and the extensive, yet still un-integrated, Pueblo Grande data and documents were threatened with an increasing probability of loss. The knowledge and software required to interface with AREV formats and to export the data grew more and more scarce with the passing of time. In addition, the hardware on which the data were stored, which was capable of running the original software programs, was growing older and more obsolete.

A collaborative project sponsored by Digital Antiquity rescued the digital data associated with several large SSI projects at Pueblo Grande. Project participants have interfaced SSI's server and hard drives with current computing hardware and extracted all of SSI's digitally stored data. In addition, they have booted the AREV database program in a Windows 7 environment and re-learned how to work with AREV to extract data tables from its relational data sets. They migrated all of the recovered data to more stable formats, creating multiple copies to ensure the long-term preservation of the original archaeological data from SSI. Moreover, the project integrates large portions of the Pueblo Grande data and curated the originals with tDAR (Thompson et al. 2012).

The Soil Systems, Inc. digital data collection faced three primary threats that may have led to data loss:

1. Data stored in non-preservation file formats, i.e. proprietary file formats that are no longer commonly used.
2. Large amounts of digitized and 'digital-born' data stored locally, on internal servers and internal hard drives.
3. Lack of resources to migrate large amounts of digital data to a curation facility/repository capable of adequately storing these data.

The problems that threatened SSI's digital data collection highlight critical issues that are common to cultural resource management and other private firm digital data archives. In most instances, private firm archaeological data are entered into, created by, and stored in widely available commercial software. At present, these data are frequently 'born' in digital environments, and are growing increasingly complex as firms have access to ever more sophisticated and powerful software packages. Although data are often backed up on servers and stored as multiple copies, they are infrequently converted to preservation-minded formats (i.e. exported from proprietary formats and into more stable, persistent formats). Second, private firm digital data are stored primarily on the hardware purchased and owned by the firm. A firm may provide copies of finalized digital data sets to an agency or repository along with its final project report for individual projects. However, these data sets likely represent only a subset of the digital data actually created during the completion of an archaeological project. In addition, the submitted digital data are often divorced from the project and site metadata when placed in a repository facility. Finally, many private firms lack available resources to undertake large-scale digital curation efforts independently on a long-term basis. In particular, these firms have almost no resources at their disposal for digital data conversion and migration when they close their businesses. Their data are then under immediate threat of obsolescence and loss.

Conclusion

The Newham Museum Service and Soil Systems, Inc. case studies describe common problems with aspects of current digital archaeological archiving practices. This guide has been developed to provide better preservation strategies for archaeological project data that will enable individuals and organizations to avoid problems and create useful and easily preserved digital data. One clear step toward improving archaeological practice in this area is recognition that the road to long-term preservation begins not at the end of a project but at its inception.

1.4 THE IMPORTANCE OF PRESERVATION AND DIGITAL ARCHIVING OF ARCHAEOLOGICAL DATA

1.4.1 The Importance of Access and Preservation

Much of the information produced by archaeological research over the past century exists in limited-distribution reports, tables, and charts scattered in offices across the nation. The data contained in these resources are often stored on magnetic tapes and floppy disks or encoded in computer cards, that are degrading in archives, museums, bookshelves, filing cabinets, or desk drawers; all the while, technology to retrieve these data – and the human knowledge required to make them meaningful – rapidly disappears (Eiteljorg 2004; McManamon et al. 2010: 2ff.; Michener et al. 1997). Museums and other repositories have typically treated the physical media on which archaeological data are recorded as artifacts and stored them as such: in boxes, on shelves.

By far the most common preservation treatment for digital data reported by repositories is to conserve the media on which the digital files are stored (McManamon and Kintigh 2010: 37; Watts 2011: 10–11). Unfortunately, this method presents serious problems. First, it renders the data on such media inaccessible unless one can physically retrieve the media, extract the data using the appropriate computer drive, and access the data with compatible software. Second, the required hardware and software for these tasks is rapidly disappearing in many cases. Third, the physical curation of the actual media (and associated hardware and software environments) is an inadequate long-term preservation approach, because both software and hardware constantly evolve and bits on magnetic and optical media gradually, but inevitably, deteriorate or 'rot'.

Current preservation practices for digital data must be improved, or a significant portion of the available information about the archaeological record will be lost. This information – collected at substantial financial, intellectual, and physical cost – must be preserved and made accessible to future generations. Present data collection practices and preservation methods, if unaltered, will render this digital data inaccessible to future investigations.

Beyond the moral and ethical reasons for ensuring proper digital preservation, often, there are also legal requirements. A significant portion of the archaeological investigations undertaken in the UK and the US involve public funding, land, permits, planning, and regulations. Typically, public agencies are responsible for overseeing these investigations and also for ensuring the preservation of important archaeological sites, collections, and associated records, which include all of the digital materials related to the investigation. In addition to being accountable for preservation, agencies must make archaeological records and data available to the public, with appropriate controls in place to protect archaeological assets. Legal frameworks requiring these actions exist in both the UK (e.g. the National Planning Policy Framework) and US (e.g. 36 CFR 79), and in many other nations.

Within existing legal frameworks, archaeological organizations, practitioners and repositories must institute good practices to ensure digital data access and long-term preservation, alongside the proper curation of physical collections and associated paper records.

1.4.2 Background to Digital Data in Archaeology

Archaeological collections consist of artifacts and associated records of the fieldwork undertaken as well as that generated during post-fieldwork recording and analysis. Many of today's recording and analytical procedures result in digital material, such as data sets, images, CAD, GIS, spreadsheets and documents. Traditionally the entire collection (artifacts, paper and digital records) would have been transferred to a museum at the end of a project's life. However, a survey into the state of museum archaeological archives in England (Swain 1998: 47), noted that 'most museums do not have the correct technology to store, access and curate in the long term those archives for which computer files form an important part'. The Swain report also highlighted that little digital material was being transferred to museums for archival purposes. This finding was echoed in *Strategies for Digital Data* (Condron et al. 1999: 6.1–6.3), which showed that the majority of digital material from archaeological projects is either retained by creators or is transferred into the hands of local government organizations. *Strategies for Digital Data* also reported that these organizations generally have inadequate policies for digital archives (Condron et al. 1999: 33–39). A similar situation seems to exist in the US, where two national surveys of archaeological repositories (Childs and Kagan 2008; Watts 2011; see also discussion in McManamon and Kintigh 2010: 37–38) suggest that digital documents and files from archaeological investigations are curated as objects rather than being made accessible. Digital archaeological material, much of which is central to description of the archaeological record, is in danger of being lost.

The intertwined problems of data access, preservation, and synthesis are not new to archaeology in the US. In the late 1990s, a series of meetings and panels were sponsored by the Society for American Archaeology, the Society of Professional Archaeologists (now the Registry of Professional Archaeologists), and the National Park Service on the general topic of 'Renewing Our National Archaeological Program'. Improving the management of archaeological information through greater data access and synthesis was one of the major topics covered in this effort (Lipe 1997; McManamon 2000).

The difficulty of preserving information about and from existing research is exacerbated by the demographic transition underway in the ranks of professional archaeologists. Large numbers of archaeologists entered the profession in the 1960s and 1970s. These individuals are now retiring or passing away (Departmental Consulting Archeologist 2010: 76–81). Figure 1.1 and Table 1.1 below show an example of this demographic process regarding the number of professional archaeologists employed by federal agencies in the US. If these projections related to retirements among federal agency archaeologists are correct, by 2017 there will be only slightly more than half the number of professional archaeologists employed by federal agencies to carry out the work being done today. Similarly, although as a result of the economic downturn of 2007, the UK has also seen a decrease in the number of professional archaeologists working in the UK alongside a loss of funding in both research and local government sectors (Aitchison 2010).

Now is the time to capture, for long-term preservation and access, the digital data associated with the work carried out by this cohort of archaeologists. Accessing the information by relying on the memories of individuals, no matter how prodigious these memories might be, will be impossible once these individuals are no longer available. Increasingly, these concerns about legacy data and preservation issues have led to an emphasis on the access to and preservation of archaeological data as an important facet of the responsible conduct of research in the discipline.

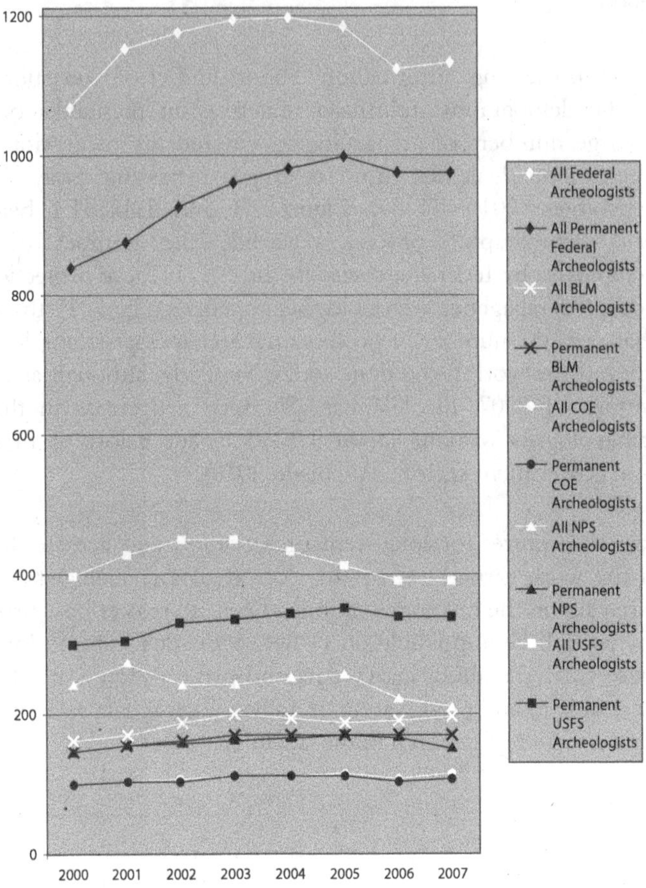

Figure 1.1: *Permanent and temporary archaeologist positions in US federal agencies, 2000–2007 (based on Departmental Consulting Archeologist 2010: figure 9)*

Table 1.1: Projected number of permanent federal agency archaeologists in 2017

Federal Agency Archaeologists (permanent)	Current[a]	New Hires[b]	Retirements[c]	Estimated Staff (2017)[d]
U.S. Forest Service	337	47	185	199
National Park Service	159	22	87	94
Bureau of Land Management	194	27	87	134
All Federal Agencies	974	136	536	574

Key:

[a] Numbers of permanent archaeologists employed by Federal agencies (as in Figure 1.1.

[b] Estimated number of archaeologists who will be hired during the ten-year period, 2007–2017, using the hiring rate for vacant NPS archaeologist positions between 2002 and 2006 as reported by the NPS Personnel Office.

[c] Estimated number of retirements of archaeologists during the ten-year period, 2007–2017, if retirements occur when retirement eligibility is reached by individuals.

[d] Estimated number calculated as: Current + New Hires – Retirements.

Data from Departmental Consulting Archeologist (2010: table 18).

The challenges of data access and preservation are not unique to archaeology. In 2009, the scientific journal *Nature* editorialized on the need for broader sharing and long-term preservation of data. The same issue of the journal included related reports on data access and preservation challenges (Nature 2009a; b; Nelson 2009; Schofield et al. 2009). The editorial cited particular successes: 'Pioneering archives such as GenBank have demonstrated just how powerful such legacy data sets can be for generating new discoveries – especially when data are combined from many laboratories and analyzed in ways that the original researchers could not have anticipated (Nature 2009a: 145)'. However, the editorial also emphasized that most scientific disciplines '...still lack the technical, institutional, and cultural frameworks required to support such open data access – leading to a scandalous shortfall in the sharing of data by researchers. This deficiency urgently needs to be addressed by funders, universities, and researchers themselves…Furthermore funding agencies need to recognize that preservation of and access to digital data are central to their mission, and need to be supported accordingly' (Nature 2009a: 145).

In 2009 the US National Academies released a book-length report on efforts to ensure the integrity, accessibility, and stewardship of digital research data (National Academies 2009). More recently, *Science* (2011) devoted a large special section to the challenges of 'Dealing with data'. Reports by experts in scientific disciplines from climatology to signal visualization reflected on how the deluge of data in their fields can be managed and used to advance knowledge.

Preserving Future Data

The challenges identified are not simply legacy issues. A substantial amount of public archaeological work is carried out annually. US federal agencies report approximately 50,000 annual field projects involving archaeological resources conducted in the United States, mostly by cultural resource management firms or agency staff (Departmental Consulting Archeologist 2009; 2010). In the UK, a recent report estimates the number of fieldwork projects carried out in 2010 to exceed 5,400 (Costen et al. 2012). Given the volume of data and reports produced each year, even archaeologists working in the same area are often unaware of important results already reported by their colleagues (e.g., see Ford 2010 for UK examples). At present, archaeological studies are accumulating a large magnitude of data, but these cannot be used efficiently and effectively to advance knowledge of the past owing to inadequate preservation practice.

Today, a great deal of background research effort is expended searching for and acquiring relevant reports. Once found, more time is required to hunt for key data in volume after volume of hard copy reports that sometimes extend to more than a thousand pages. Yet, the ability to access and reanalyze existing data can make present-day investigations more productive and has the potential to identify and reduce costly redundant projects.

1.4.3 Resource Discovery and Reuse

As a profession, archaeology is heavily dependent on knowledge of, and access to, reports and data from previous investigations. Furthermore, one critical aspect of preservation is dissemination or, following the old adage, 'lots of copies keep stuff safe'. The Swain report (1998, 43–45) looked into the usage of archaeological collections and concluded that they were a grossly under-utilized resource. Reasons for this under-use may include difficulty in locating information about collections' contents as well as the dispersal of finds and documentary material to different repositories. The development of appropriate resource discovery tools is of fundamental importance in helping potential users not only to find the material they require, enabling reuse of digital resources, but also to direct them toward repositories containing the material of interest.

At present, potential user communities are largely unaware of the digital resources available. Making basic information about archaeological archives available at the earliest possible opportunity through a resource discovery tool like ArchSearch, the online catalogue of the ADS, or tDAR, the digital repository of Digital Antiquity, increases awareness and improves potential reuse. ArchSearch and tDAR demonstrate different approaches to providing access.

> **ADS (Archaeology Data Service – http://archaeologydataservice.ac.uk)** holdings are split between the site-level 'monument inventories', searchable via ArchSearch, and the data 'archives' section with its own separate search mechanism. Both areas of the site employ a faceted classification system, allowing users to search each section via free text keywords and then narrow down results via a series of categories or 'facets'. For ArchSearch site level data, these facets fall into the familiar categories of what, where, and when, with the various sub-facets coming from standardized lists such as the Monument Type Thesaurus. ArchSearch users can additionally narrow down searches by resource type or by using a map interface to constrain the search to a specific area. ADS archives can similarly be searched using subject, region, and program facets.

> **tDAR (the Digital Archaeological Record – http://tdar.org)** is digital resource- or project-specific rather than being organized by site. Searches within tDAR will discover projects, documents, images, data sets, or other digital resources associated with any given search. Users may search by map, keyword, culture, time period, or even based on the text within a document or in the metadata description for a document, image, or data set. tDAR includes citation, geographic location, and brief descriptive data about over 365,000 archaeological reports in the US. For a growing number of records, a digital copy of the document also is available. A preliminary search of tDAR can provide an initial understanding of the archaeological investigations already done in any particular area. With this basic information, researchers can begin to locate reports of these investigations and other studies in their area of interest.

Too often, repositories are seen as the final resting place for archaeological information, rather than as one stage in a cycle of information gathering and reuse. As Swain (1998: 14) notes, 'it has also been accepted for many years that archaeological techniques and technology will improve through time to extract new information from material that may not be possible at present'. Archives form a vital and living part of the archaeological resource and should be queried during later research projects. Current government planning guidance in the UK and archaeological resource management policies in the US emphasize a preference for preservation as opposed to excavation, so increasingly, the role of the archaeological collection is moving to center stage (see articles in Childs (2010) for a similar perspective and examples in the US). In order to define appropriate management and investigation strategies, existing collections must be consulted.

Archaeological publication of fieldwork projects is moving away from traditional large monographs towards the 'slim volume' or a synthetic summary of the fieldwork. Such a development increases the importance of the digital archive, which may well become the only source for primary data. This form of publication has been chosen for numerous projects including the Fyfield and Overton Downs project (Fowler 2000a) which is an integrated monograph and internet publication (Fowler 2000b) in which readers are able to move from the high-level interpretations contained in the monograph to the minutiae of the data held in the online digital archive. Projects such as *Making the LEAP* and *LEAP II* (Internet Archaeology 2012) have further extended this idea and linked online publications with their associated digital archives.

There is new, broader interest in archaeological information at all levels, local, regional, national, and international. In part, this is fed by growing access to the Internet and increasing curiosity about family research and local history. New inquiries and perspectives come with this widening public scrutiny, and bring with them new stimuli for archaeologists to review the way that data and associated interpretations are recorded and disseminated. We no longer operate in a world where archaeological data are created by archaeologists for archaeologists. As digitization and computer literacy increase, the archaeological record will become more accessible and public. In the US, public policy generally favors wide access to information, especially if that information has been generated by publicly funded or required activities (Open Government Initiative 2012), like so much of the archaeological investigations undertaken in the US. In particular, the National Historic Preservation Act (Section 1 and Section 112(a)(2), see also ACHP 2008), the Antiquities Act (Section 3), the Archaeological Resources Protection Act (Sections 10(c) and 11), and the government-wide regulations, 36 CFR 79 require substantial public access to archaeological information (Cultural Heritage Partners 2012).

Finally, ease of access and improved ability to share digital archaeological data provides new opportunities for scholarly and scientific research across national boundaries. Digital gateways like ARENA2 (Archaeology Data Service 2012a), and TAG (Archaeology Data Service 2012b) represent the future potential of these repositories and tools – enabling centralized discovery of resources from around the world.

1.5 APPROACHES TO DIGITAL ARCHIVING

1.5.1 Choosing an Archive

This section provides data creators and depositors with the information to assess whether a specific archive is suitable for their data. In certain circumstances, depending on the nature of the project, the funding body, or the digital data created, a specific digital archive may be recommended as the final destination for a project's digital output. The standards discussed below describe the procedures necessary for maintaining digital archives and repositories. The requirements outlined in these standards are established to ensure that data archived in repositories that adhere to the standards remains secure and accessible for the long term. In short, a digital archive should be able to 'provide reliable, long-term access to managed digital resources to its designated community, now and in the future' (RLG 2002: 5).

Organizations responsible for the long-term preservation and management of digital data should have well-documented archival strategies and procedures in place. Documentation can range from generic to specific policy statements, for example, the series of Preservation Handbooks produced by the UK's Arts and Humanities Data Service (AHDS) and its subject-specific data centers, including the ADS (Arts and Humanities Data Service 2006). Other national and international organizations providing useful guidelines on archiving strategies and procedures include the UK Data Archive (UKDA), the British Library (2012), the Library of Congress (2012a), NASA's National Space Science Data Center (NSSDC 2012), the Electronic Resource Preservation and Access Network (ERPANET), The Digital Preservation Coalition (DPC) and the Digital Curation Centre (DCC).

In addition to available documentation, most archives require depositors to complete formal agreements or licenses when depositing data. Such agreements should detail the archive's responsibilities together with any responsibilities placed on the depositor (e.g. clearance of relevant copyrights). Such agreements are an essential part of archive certification standards and provide a concise outline of the level of service provided to the depositor by the archive.

Standards

One of the primary standards for digital archiving is The Open Archival Information System (OAIS) reference model (Consultative Committee for Space Data Systems 2012). The OAIS model is a set of criteria and practices that are recommended to ensure long-term preservation of digital information. The model provides a common framework of terms and concepts that is intended to be applicable to any number of disciplines or subject matters. The model takes a holistic approach to digital preservation, focusing not only on the technical infrastructure, but also ensuring the social and organizational environment is set up to ensure digital preservation. The model provides a 'framework' for setting up a digital archive as opposed to an explicit set of instructions. Over time, this model has become one of the central tenets of certification as a recognized digital repository. Individual digital archives can demonstrate compliance with the OAIS reference model through the process of certification. However, such audit checklists are a very recent development and many digital archives are in the process of meeting certification requirements.

Certification

Recently two separate initiatives have begun to certify repositories: the *Trustworthy Repositories Audit & Certification (TRAC) Checklist*, and the *Data Seal of Approval.* Both were initially published in 2007, but take different approaches to certification. One certification document has been published as *Trustworthy Repositories Audit & Certification (TRAC): Criteria and Checklist* (Center for Research Libraries (CRL) et al. 2007), by the US-based Research Libraries Group (RLG), the Center for Research Libraries (CRL) and the United States National Archives and Records Administration (NARA). The publication provides a checklist of policies and procedures that repositories need to follow in order to be capable of reliably managing and preserving digital collections. The audit checklist is closely tied to the OAIS reference model in its conceptual framework and terminology. It considers organizational suitability, repository workflows, user communities and the usability of data, plus the overarching policies and underlying technical infrastructure of a repository, including security. All of these areas must be openly documented. Organizations that can demonstrate that they meet the criteria within the checklist will be identified as 'trusted digital repositories'. The CRL undertakes projects to evaluate the *TRAC* system and has several reports on these projects (CRL 2012), and has published a number of audit reports on their website including one for the digital journal archive Portico (CRL 2012).

The Data Seal of Approval (2012) led by the Data Archiving and Network Services group for the Netherlands (DANS), UK Data Archive, the University of Michigan and other European partners provide a similar quality assessment to that of the TRAC system, although with a slightly simpler structure based on sixteen guidelines and focused on three groups of stakeholders (producer, consumer and archive). Again, as with TRAC, the aim is to 'guarantee the durability of the data concerned, but also to promote the goal of durable archiving in general'.

1.5.2 Archival Strategies and Digital Lifecycles

Although it is easy to ignore issues of digital archaeological data preservation until the near-completion of a project, it is critical to consider the preservation strategy as part of project planning and throughout a project's lifecycle. At a minimum, documentation should catalogue all of the contextual information necessary to use the materials in the future, including translations of codes and abbreviations used in descriptive or analytical data sets, as well as descriptions of how data were captured. Depending on the preservation strategy selected, different resources may need to be identified to ensure preservation and access beyond the life of the project.

The three most common digital preservation strategies are:

1. Technology preservation – where the hardware and software required to access and use the data must be maintained and preserved along with it.
2. Emulation – where special software is used to emulate the hardware environment and operating system to run the software that originally produced and uses the data.
3. Migration – where the data is migrated over time to be compatible with later versions of the software, or ideally, to open standards such as PDF/A or TIFF that can be more universally accessed.

Each of these strategies involves different requirements for what is archived and documented. Specific hardware descriptions, software version numbers, license keys and copies, as well as documentation of processes for saving and exporting files or using software are important candidates for documentation and archiving. Both Digital Antiquity and ADS rely on the migration model for digital preservation. This model ideally creates less work and need for infrastructure in the long term, because serious preservation issues are identified and addressed at the time of data ingest. At that point, both the original and a preservation format of the file are archived.

When selecting an archive, it is important to evaluate the archival policies and procedures of possible repositories. An important part of this process is to ensure that the policies of a potential repository cover preservation, access, backups, migrations, disaster recovery and sustainability.

Evaluating the Three Digital Preservation Strategies

The preservation of digital files can be broken down into two key elements: first, the continued storage of data in an accessible and robust format, and second, the creation and maintenance of documentation (metadata) that allows the preserved data to be understood. Digital archiving strategies do not, and should not, rely simply on the physical preservation of a single disk, tape, or CD/DVD-ROM. The preservation of digital data, regardless of subject area or content, is generally approached via one of three main strategies, technology preservation, emulation and migration.

It is recommended that a migration-based approach be adopted for the preservation of archaeological digital data. Such an approach relies on the periodic migration of information from older hardware and software to newer systems. Conversely, in a technology preservation strategy, the data are maintained unchanged along with the technology (hardware and/or software) upon which it depends. Rothenberg (1999: section 6.3) raises a number of problems associated with such a reliance on 'computer museums', namely that technology will inevitably fail over time, while maintenance and replacement simultaneously become increasingly difficult and costly. In the context of many archaeological projects, it is likely that substantial amounts of very specific software and hardware would need to be documented and preserved. The complete conservation and continual maintenance of obsolete hardware and software systems, as part of technology preservation, is a costly and high-risk strategy. Adopting such a strategy would seem to be unjustifiable unless data cannot be migrated and are of substantial international importance.

An emulation strategy attempts to avoid some of the pitfalls of technology preservation through the emulation of older hardware or software systems in newer ones. This is technically challenging, expensive, and becomes increasingly difficult as technology develops and progresses, becoming ever more remote from the original systems employed. Emulation is therefore not recommended for archaeological archives.

Preservation by Migration

A migration-based preservation strategy focuses on moving data to software-independent formats (normalization) and subsequently migrating that data through successive technical infrastructures over time (refreshment). There is a preference within the archival community that data should be migrated to a small set of stable file formats and that this process be openly documented. This reduces the potential number of refreshments that the data have to undergo and allows migration processes to be carried out easily across large sets of data. It is recommended that digital archiving in archaeology should employ the policies and procedures of controlled data migration.

Excluding data refreshment, the copying of information from one medium to the next as it reaches the end of its reliable life span, there are two additional key activities required for successful digital archiving within a migration strategy: data migration and data documentation.

Data Migration

Data migration is the act of copying digital information from one format or structure into another that can be read by current versions of software. One example is the migration of data between different Computer-Aided Design (CAD) packages. However, even though CAD packages allow data to be exported in a 'standard' format (DXF), in fact many programs create such DXF files in unique ways, so that other packages may not be able to read them. The unwary can find that, without careful migration, much of the original information is lost when creating a new file. Many migration programs incorporate a process of format normalization: files are migrated to common, stable formats and then, when necessary, through successive versions of the format. An ideal is to normalize files to open-standard and preferably text-based formats (e.g. XML or ASCII), although this is not always an option; for instance images. In such cases, version and format migration is practiced, and files in these formats are also subject to periodic refreshment.

The data migration strategy requires that all file formats being stored within a repository are tracked and commonly that only certain formats are accepted by the repository. Formats that are selected are either open standards and/or widely used file formats as the standards for accessing and preservation. For example, while PDF/A is an archival standard, at some point in the future, it may no longer be the *de facto* standard and become difficult to open or use. At such point, PDF/A documents within the archive would be migrated to a more modern equivalent. Migration procedures developed in common with other digital archives are expected to reduce the administrative and technical procedures required when such migration efforts become necessary.

It is also essential to monitor ongoing research and development into good digital preservation strategies, and not to assume that the same formats are always the safest. Digital preservation requires active intervention and constant vigilance. If this cannot be provided locally, it is best to contact a professional digital archiving service. A strict regime of validating all files and their documentation must be followed during the migration process. Original media should be retained until the validation process is

100% complete since it may be necessary to return to the original file if any aspect of the data could not be successfully and safely migrated.

Data Documentation

In order for a digital archivist to migrate digital information successfully, it is necessary to understand the structure of the data and how different parts relate to one another. Data migration thus relies on an additional activity: data documentation.

Documentation is essential for both the preservation and reuse of all data types. For example, although their creator might understand abbreviations and shorthand used in the data, there is no guarantee that these will make sense to someone reusing the data several years later. Worse still, in a large archive, a file describing contexts or small finds may relate to only one of several possible excavations. For these reasons, it is necessary to document the codes or abbreviations used in the data together with any standards that have been followed or thesauri or word lists that have been used. In addition, it is often useful to provide an accurate (if brief) description of each file, explaining how different files fit together. Software often incorporates the option to generate documentation during the creation of files (e.g., field descriptions in databases), though these options can vary in their depth and relevance. The type of documentation required will also depend on the type of data; for example, the documentation for a text file may be quite straightforward, while that for a GIS or database may be quite intensive. Data documentation, at the file or data type level, is dealt with in more detail in Part 2 of this guide.

No digital archivist can successfully preserve data that are not fully documented, because at every step of data migration information can be lost. This leaves archivists with two options: migrating data from one format and then double-checking each entry manually, or requiring thorough documentation of the data at the time of archiving so migrations can be carefully planned and tested in advance.

The Digital Lifecycle

Preservation of digital data by data migration – the strategy advocated by this guide – together with the OAIS model (Consultative Committee for Space Data Systems 2012) places an emphasis on the ongoing management and administration of a digital resource and the object lifecycle.

Although simplified, the generally recognized categories of the lifecycle of digital assets are:

1. Data creation.
2. Documentation and metadata.
3. Acquisition and selection (retention or disposal).
4. Preservation and management.
5. Access and use/reuse.

The concept of a digital object lifecycle has been around for some time. At the 2006 conference 'The LIFE Project: Bringing digital preservation to life', Neil Beagrie (2006) gave a paper entitled 'Life cycle modelling: the background', in which he discussed the evolution of lifecycle management from its beginnings in publications such as the *Terotechnology Handbook* (1978), which considered lifecycle costing and the idea of 'total cost of ownership' for physical objects. Subsequently, during the 1990s, the AHDS, the British Library and others built on this approach for digital assets. Beagrie noted how the early involvement of the UK's Joint Information Systems Committee (JISC) and the AHDS with project proposals, through the provision of guidance and advice, helped to reduce costs downstream. One manifestation of this early involvement was the publication of a number of the *Guides to Good Practice* (Arts and Humanities Data Service 2007).

The Digital Curation Centre's Curation Lifecycle Model (2008) provides a concise overview of how an object lifecycle can function and how elements continually feed back into the processes of preservation and reuse.

Part 2. Planning for the Creation of Digital Data

2.1 DATA CREATION AND CAPTURE: GENERAL ISSUES

From the moment a project begins, careful thought must go into the planning of the digital materials that will be created throughout the project's lifecycle. Basic planning at the beginning of the process will significantly simplify the submission of project materials to a digital archive when the project is completed. Initial planning will also help ensure data security and recovery throughout the lifecycle of the project. Issues to consider include the types and estimated numbers and size of digital files that will be archived for the project. Additionally, file naming, versioning, as well as storage, backup strategies, and documentation should be planned for ahead of archiving. This section contains more detailed discussions of all these issues.

Before planning, decide exactly where to archive digital materials. If materials are to be contributed to an existing digital repository, contact that repository during the planning stage of the project to review the issues described in this section. This will be helpful in selecting the appropriate repository for data and simplify the submission process.

Although project planning is often specific to the project and data types being generated (and will be covered within the technique-specific chapters that follow), some general project planning principles apply regardless of project type. While planning a project, consider the following issues:

- **Choose what to archive and where the project archive will be deposited for long-term care**:
    - **Preparing a project design** that defines the types of digital data that will be created or acquired and who is responsible for creating and managing these files during the project.
    - **Selecting the file formats** that will be used during the data creation and analysis phases, and how these relate to formats used in the archiving and dissemination of data. The formats used may be the same or may change during the project lifecycle.
- **Determine the level of documentation and metadata required** at the various levels (project, technique, file) to ensure that the project and the digital files created are understandable and reusable. This is covered in the sections below on Project Documentation and Metadata.
- **Choosing how to archive**:
    - **Decide upon the type of digital files** that will be created and which files will be preserved. This is covered in the sections on Data Selection and Storage.
    - **Decide upon what to archive.** Estimate the number of files and storage required to archive your project. This can be important in

evaluating the overall cost of archiving, as well as strategies for working with the data.

- **Contact the digital archive facility** destined to receive the files to see which specific guidelines or standards should be followed. If guidelines are not specified, it is recommended that the advice in this Guide be followed.

Most importantly, include in project plans the tasks necessary for the creation and documentation of the digital data files that will accurately and clearly describe the project and its results. The project plan must include steps to ensure that these files are placed in a digital repository where they will be accessible and preserved for future use.

2.1.1 File Formats

This subsection outlines general issues that should be considered when assessing general file formats. Part 3 of this guide covers specific file formats and software applications commonly used during the data creation phase, which are discussed in terms of their suitability for long-term preservation and possible migration paths to other formats.

Open and Proprietary Formats and Standards

There is a general preference among digital archives and repositories to store data in formats that are standardized, openly documented and, where possible, non-proprietary. Such formats are considered to be more easily sustainable due to the openness and availability of the file format and, in many cases, its use across platforms or by multiple applications. This is discussed elsewhere (Library of Congress 2012a and Todd 2009) in terms of disclosure, external dependencies, impact of patents and adoption.

Binary and Plain Text Files

Most computer files are not 'human-readable', i.e. files composed of plain text. Binary files are digital files that have some structure or encoding. Examples of such files are images, databases, and even word-processing documents and, for many of these, file formats based on binary encoding are the only options. However, for a wide range of data sets, such as spreadsheets, databases, text documents and so on, there is generally an option (and for an archive, a preference) to use a file format based on plain-text encoding (e.g., ASCII plain text or XML). The advantages are that the file format is more transparent (i.e. it is human-readable and more open to direct analysis) and, as a result, more likely to be identified in terms of content and associated software. Easy access to file content also means that such formats have fewer external dependencies and more possible migration paths, key factors for long-term preservation, should the associated software become unavailable.

Compressed Files

File compression is often used for two purposes: to reduce the actual size of the files (e.g., JPG or TIFF files) or to group multiple files together (e.g., a ZIP file). In both cases, the compression can either be lossless (i.e., no data is discarded) or lossy (i.e., where some data, often invisible to the human eye, may be discarded). Lossy compression used within a file format, such as JPG images or MPEG video, can cause additional problems and degradation of data quality – known as 'generation loss' – when files are continuously reprocessed and recompressed (Heydegger 2008). In the case of single 'archive' files, as with binary encoding, data compression creates a potential barrier to identifying file types and accessing content.

While certain formats, like binary or compressed files, may not be suitable for long-term preservation, they may be the most appropriate for data creation, development and dissemination (Brown 2008a: 5). It is recommended that such considerations be recognized in the data creation stage of a project so that adequate planning can be put in place – if required – for the later conversion of possibly problematic files into digital files that are more susceptible to long-term preservation and accessibility and use by others.

Format Popularity and Adoption

An important element that is key to identifying a suitable file format is the level of *adoption*, i.e. how commonly is a specific file format used by the larger community of archaeologists and archaeological organizations as well as the broader community of practice. The extent to which particular file formats are common can vary between techniques, data types and countries.

There are a number of resources available that describe in detail the criteria used to identify suitable digital formats for preservation. Examples include those published by the Library of Congress (2012a), The National Archives in the UK (Brown 2008a) and the Digital Preservation Coalition (2012). Figure 2.1 describes some of the basic stages used in selecting a suitable preservation format.

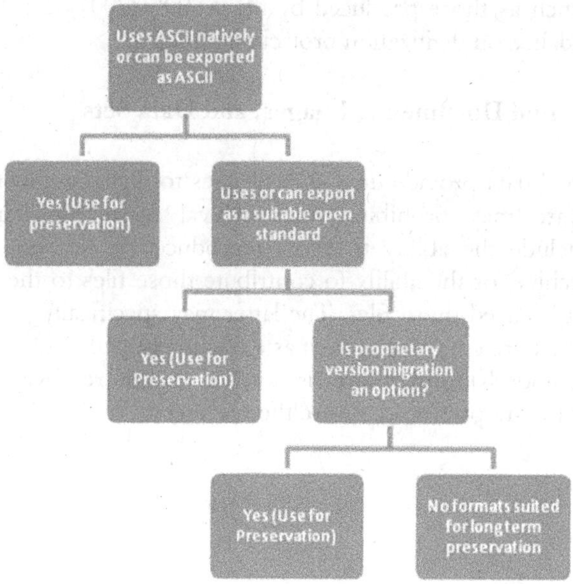

Figure 2.1: *The main stages involved in the selection of a data format that is suitable for preservation*

2.1.2 Data Sources

Distinctions should be made early on in a project between data created digitally ('born digital') and that captured from a non-digital original (digitized).

Digitized Data

As with the online *Guides*, this publication focuses on *born-digital* data and does not aim to provide detailed advice on digitization. However, projects that include digitization of paper records, whether digitizing in-house or outsourcing such work, should still consider the implications of file formats. Regardless of format, such projects should plan to digitize original material, for example, paper or film, using the highest quality data capture to create archival-quality digital data files. It may be advisable to create and store multiple versions of each file, some for dissemination and others for long-term archiving. The originals from which the digital data were created may still be useful, and a documentary archive should be consulted to establish whether this information should be preserved in physical form.

Substantial guidance is available regarding digitization. JISC Digital Media provide a wide range of advice on digitizing existing images as well as analogue audio and video.

Other guidelines, such as those produced by the AHDS (2007) and UKOLN (2004) provide shorter guidance on digitization project planning.

Licensed and External Documents, Images, and Data Sets

Licensed and external data provide unique challenges to digital archiving as copyright, licenses, or software may prohibit some archival tasks. Challenges related to proprietary data include the ability to copy, reproduce, or convert files from their formats into the archive, or the ability to contribute those files to the archive because the archive has not licensed those files. The latter may specifically be challenging, for example with files that are composites such as a document with embedded images or a GIS file where the underlying map layer is licensed and its removal will significantly diminish the ability to interpret, read, or use the file later.

2.2 PRACTICAL ADVICE

2.2.1 File Naming Conventions

Regardless of the source of the data, one of the first (and most immediate) ways of ensuring that data can be understood is to use meaningful file names that reflect content. Plan to use standard file naming conventions and directory structures from the beginning of a project and, where possible, use consistent conventions across all projects. Directory structures and file names are discussed in relation to specific types of data in a number of the following chapters, but general principles and conventions to consider are:

- Reserve the 3- or 4-letter file extension for application-specific codes, e.g. PDF, DOCX, TIF appropriate for that file format, and avoid using a full stop/period (.) elsewhere in a file name.
- Where possible, avoid using spaces within filenames, as they can cause problems in some operating systems. Use the underscore character (_) to imply a space within the filename.
- Include some means of identifying the relevant activity in the file name, e.g., a unique reference number, project number, or project name.
- Include version number information in the file name where necessary.
- Be aware that files generated under certain operating systems may have specific requirements, e.g., MS-DOS filenames are restricted to 11 characters whereas long file names may be used under a Windows environment. Some operating systems, such as Unix, are also case-sensitive with the result that 'File.txt' and 'file.txt' would be recognized as different files.

2.2.2 Version Control

It is extremely important to maintain strict version control when working with files, especially if different people are working on single files or if files undergo multiple stages of processing.

There are three common strategies for providing version control:

- File naming conventions.
- Standard headers listing creation dates and version numbers.
- File logs.

It is important to record, where practical, every change to a file no matter how small the change. Versions that are no longer needed should be removed after ensuring that adequate backup files have been created.

2.2.3 Storage and Backup

During the working life of most projects, digital data will be created on the hard disks of standalone PCs, on laptop computers or on network drives. Additionally, data may be acquired or stored on USB drives, backup tapes, CDs, DVDs, or other electronic media. Ideally, regardless of how they were created or acquired, digital files in current use will be routinely backed up as part of good working practice.

It is not sufficient to store digital media on shelves or file cabinets. Fireproof, anti-magnetic facilities are extremely important for the safe storage of digital media, and backup versions should be stored separated from original media. Ensure that the archive is complete and that documentation is included before storing it away. It is also important to employ an effective data management system in which file storage locations and media labeling strategies are noted.

Secure Backup

Backup is the familiar task of ensuring that there is an emergency copy, or snapshot, of data held somewhere other than the primary location. For a small project, this may mean a single file held on an external disc drive or over a network or the Internet. For a larger project it may require more rigorous procedures of disaster planning, with fireproof cupboards, off-site copies and daily, weekly and monthly copy creation. These are important in the lifespan of the project, but are not the same as long-term archiving because once the project is completed and its digital archive safely deposited in a digital repository, the action of backing up will become unnecessary.

For small or relatively static data, regular copying and backup may be excessive, and the following advice should be tuned to follow actual use. For a larger project, the most widely used backup strategy is the so-called 'Grandparent–Parent–Child' strategy. The system works by employing a rotation of full and partial backups on each day of the week or month. The most recent full backup, the 'Parent', contains a snapshot of the whole project or set of data at the start of a week. 'Children' are more frequent, normally daily, backups containing only the changes to the system executed on that day. These smaller backups don't have to be kept in perpetuity, but can be recycled every time a new Parent is created. Once a month or so, a permanent and complete snapshot is taken, which should be stored in perpetuity and would not normally be recycled. This monthly backup is the 'Grandparent' and can be relied upon in moments of real crisis. It is best practice that the weekly and monthly backups are stored offsite, preferably in a secure, fireproof, anti-magnetic environment.

It is also important to validate backup copies to ensure that all formatting and important data have been accurately preserved. Create backups when a project is complete or dormant, prior to any major changes, or if files are large enough to cause handling difficulties on the network. Each backup should be clearly named and its location should be logged.

Periodic Checking for Viruses and Other Issues

Periodic checks should be performed on a random sample of digital files, whether in active use or stored elsewhere. Appropriate checks include searching for viruses and routine screening procedures included in most computer operating systems. These periodic checks should be in addition to constant, rigorous virus searching on all files.

Additional Threats

The creation of secure backup copies does not adequately protect digital data in the long term. Threats to the data include the degradation of the media on which they are stored or changes in the hardware or the software that was used to create or use the files leading to the data becoming irretrievable. Additional steps are required for successful digital archiving.

Media Lifespan

It is critical to understand and plan for the eventual failure of ALL backup and primary media. CDs, DVDs, flash drives, disks, tapes, hard drives – even punch cards have a lifespan. CDs and DVDs are susceptible to scratching, damage by heat, and eventual failure of the dyes and plastic that store the data. Hard drives may be damaged by magnets or fail due to numerous mechanical or environmental causes. Regardless of the media on which you're storing files, you must plan for the eventual failure of all backup and primary media by creating additional backups and migrating to new media. Life span estimates vary, but more information on the issues of media lifespan can be found in Brown (2008b) together with various US National Archives FAQs (National Archives 2007; n.d.).

2.2.4 Planning for Long-Term Data Curation

This section outlines the main requirements and issues concerning the long-term preservation and dissemination of archaeological documents, data sets, images, and other resources. It is assumed throughout this guide that data creators will ultimately deposit materials with a suitable digital archive or repository. A number of factors need to be considered when evaluating an archive or preparing a project for deposit. Such factors include storage, backup, bandwidth, access, and the size or complexity of the data, for example, the results of 3-D or long-range sensory data scans.

Storage

Planning for storage, backup, and dissemination may be simple, depending on the amount and lifecycle of project data. However, aspects of the data lifecycle may grow over time or through the amount or complexity of data collected and some of these issues may become more complicated. For projects that span more than a few years, hardware replacement and migration costs should be considered. Furthermore, larger projects will require additional infrastructure to ensure appropriate storage, backup, and dissemination. Although initial purchase may be expensive, over time, storage is often comparatively cheap and its cost may be considered negligible over a 20-year period when compared to other costs.

For projects with significant amounts of data, network infrastructure may also be important; like archives, data transfer (for backups, dissemination, or storage) will become a factor in the ability of a project to succeed. In certain cases, the use of physical media and the calculation of checksums when transferring files, especially large data files, may be useful to ensure the speed and accuracy of transfer.

Backup and Data Curation

On the surface, the physical storage of most files is largely unproblematic with terabyte external hard drives cheaply and widely available. A basic strategy that could be utilized for any project could be as simple as the use of high-capacity hard drives, with copies stored offsite in a fairly inert environment and synchronized on a regular basis with the master data. Such a strategy should be supported, as previously outlined, by other procedures to ensure reliable version control and protection from viruses and other sources of data corruption.

Many archival organizations, however, invest heavily in backing up data (both internally and externally), as they have different needs from small projects. For example, the ADS maintains two separate backups for its data: it subscribes to the University of York backup service, which uses Legato Networker and an Adic Scalar

Tape Library, and also maintains copies of data in the UK Data Archive (UKDA). Digital Antiquity also uses a multi-tier backup system with on- and off-site backups provided by Arizona State University, while additional backups are archived and stored in a separate off-site location.

Data Refreshment

Eventually all media will fail. Backup strategies should not only include backup plans, but plans to replace – or refresh – the storage media and hardware according to their projected lifespans. While the cost of physical 'per megabyte, gigabyte, etc.' storage continues to decrease, data refreshment and long-term curation activities – manual tasks that cannot be automated but are key factors in continuing to make data accessible and available – remain as fixed costs. Additionally, aside from the possibility of failure of storage systems, archives may choose periodically to upgrade systems or parts thereof in order to take advantage of technological advances and decreasing costs in certain areas.

2.2.5 File Organization

Digital files should also be organized into easily understandable directory structures. It may be desirable to collect related data files in a folder using standard naming conventions to aid retrieval from the directory structure. Some files, produced as the result of certain techniques (e.g., geophysical survey or GIS), are best structured and stored in standardized file structures and these are discussed in Part 3 of this guide and in the relevant sections of the online *Guides to Good Practice.*

2.3 DATA SELECTION

Selection and retention is a complex topic and a common issue for both physical and digital archives. While it may be cost-effective to select only certain files for archiving, different files or versions may become more important to future researchers, and new tools might enable better analysis of existing data. For complex data types, such as sensory scans or video recordings, these issues become critical as raw data may undergo significant changes when transformed into the final product. In contrast, on a modern investigation, it may be impossible, imprudent, or unhelpful to archive all of the digital images captured in the excavation, as pictures may be out-of-focus, of inappropriate subject matter, or simply duplicate existing material. Due to the time, costs, and resources involved, it is often important to discuss data selection issues with your selected archive early in your project to plan appropriately.

Preservation Intervention Points

The concept of a 'preservation intervention point' identifies specific points in time to archive data either right before and/or right after it is changed significantly. Examples might include: a site plan, with thousands of GPS points, layers, and shapes that may change constantly over the life of the site, a faunal database that changes throughout the excavation and may undergo larger scale changes through its lifespan, or a LIDAR or 3-D scan which must undergo a series of transformations as it is analyzed.

Preservation intervention points provide a 'chain of evidence' for data and, ideally, allow for the capture of the source, the result, and the processes or methods that ensure the transformation is repeatable. Although preservation intervention points are clearly more applicable to complex data types, they are still important for other source materials, such as images, where processing raw data can cause significant changes in the final result.

For complex data capture or analysis tasks, copies of the data should be selected for archive after each significant step of the process. The notion of data selection needs special attention, particularly in a complex archaeological project where data are acquired through one or multiple techniques and then merged or reprocessed through a number of phases to create a final 'product'. Where a project has a series of lifecycle stages such as decimation, aggregation, recasting, and annotation, through which data are transformed, as well as being migrated from format to format, then there may be more than one potential preservation intervention point.

Data documentation and metadata are also key components of the preservation intervention point concept. Although it is generally considered good practice that data should be in as raw a state as possible for preservation, on the assumption that any subsequent transformations applied can be re-created with the right documentation, this is not the case for all types of data.

The online versions of these guides cover preservation intervention points in significantly more detail.

In addition to the nature of the data itself, issues such as file size, storage costs, copyright and confidentiality may influence what data are selected for the final project archive. These issues are covered elsewhere in this guide.

2.4 PROJECT DOCUMENTATION

When archaeologists think of 'documentation' they generally think of the reports presenting information about the project's history, archaeological background and results. Such documentation is a vital component of any archaeological project. But, in order for the digital data from a project to be truly reusable, more specialized forms of technical documentation – or metadata – also are required. Such structured metadata (i.e. data about data) range from broadly applicable project-level information such as the project name, location and duration down to metadata specific to a data set or file, for instance which file formats are in the archive and which applications were used to create them. A succinct summary of both documentation and metadata can be found on the UK Data Archive website (UK Data Archive 2012):

> **Documentation:** explains how data were created or digitized, what data mean, what their content and structure are, and any manipulations that may have taken place.
>
> **Metadata:** are a subset of core data documentation, which describes the information contained in a digital resource and the characteristics of the resources. For example, for a digital text metadata would include a title, author, an abstract or description, as well as some standardized, structured information describing the purpose, origin, time references, geographic location, creator, access conditions and terms of use of a data collection.

The creation of documentation and metadata should be an ongoing process throughout the lifecycle of the project and not just an event that occurs at the end or at the point of deposition with an archive. This section describes the types and level of documentation for archaeological projects. The following section highlights the types of metadata, including specific schema and standards that are required to aid in the discovery, preservation and reuse of archaeological data.

2.4.1 Key Elements of Documentation

A summary description of the project, including its purpose, objectives, results, and other important background is needed and any special circumstances relating to why or how the project was carried out should also be included in the summary. The potential reuse of digital data makes it particularly important that this information is clearly reported. A digital copy of the project proposal or contract, with proprietary and other confidential information omitted, might also be included in the digital archive to provide this information.

Methodology

Project archives should include digital copies of site recording guidance or manuals, bibliographic references to publications describing the methodologies used as part of the project, along with any details of how recording systems have been used within the specific project. An example would be descriptions of how spatial and/or stratigraphic units were defined. Descriptions should be provided about the use of context, layer and feature numbering systems, including details of site codes, coding sheets, and area numbers; the allocation of blocks of context numbers to specific areas of the site; blocks of numbers not used, and so on. Documentation should describe any codes used, providing their expansions, with reference to any standard systems or controlled vocabulary that has been used.

Any sampling strategies that have been employed on site or in post-excavation analysis should be fully documented, as these will be particularly important to allow the reuse of artifact and environmental data. For example, layers that have been sampled or wet or dry sieved should be documented along with precise details of the sampling methodology employed. Where standard recovery levels are employed these should be documented. The strategy for defining small and bulk finds also needs documenting.

The strategy for production of the drawn record requires documentation, including details of drawing scales, and whether a system of single or multi-context plans was employed on site. Details of the site grid and its relationship to the national grid should be recorded, as well as the site datum and its relationship to height above sea level. In addition, for topographic survey, drawing details of the survey strategy need to be documented, such as whether points were taken at the top and bottom of slopes or, if on a regular grid, what grid size was used.

Site Narrative and Historical/Archaeological Context

It is important to provide bibliographic references to the appropriate excavation or fieldwork publication, but it is also important that a summary is included as part of the digital archive. In the case of excavation projects it is assumed that for most project archives the full site report, or reports in the case of large projects, will be deposited in digital format. It will also be valuable for potential reuse of the digital data if any particular strengths or weaknesses of the data are highlighted as part of the summary.

Additional Documentation

This consists of any additional texts that will facilitate and enhance the preservation and reuse of data from a project digital archive. It could include published reports, grey literature reports, correspondence, notes, or scanned field or laboratory notebooks.

2.5 METADATA

Metadata is descriptive information about documents, data sets, images, and other digital objects. Providing metadata enables discovery, accessibility, and usability of files contributed to a digital archive by providing general and standardized fields and terms to describe files and the information they contain. Furthermore, metadata provides context for non-textual materials such as data sets or images that may not be usable without this additional information. Metadata refers to a standardized set (a scheme or schema) of information that can be used to document, in a structured way. Put simply, metadata aims to make digital resources easily identifiable, retrievable and usable through the storage of descriptive and contextual information.

Depending on the project, resource, or file, metadata may be either general or specific, but at minimum should provide the 'who, what, when, where and how' information relating to a file or project. Information should be detailed enough that others are able to evaluate from the metadata whether they need the file or project. Common types of metadata include:

- General descriptive information about the contents of a file or project.
- Information that places the project or file within a broader context.
- Administrative information tracking submission, access, and rights.
- Technical metadata identifying how the file was created, the program used, file size, and other detailed information.

The process and reasons for creating metadata are well documented in a number of existing guidelines and by numerous organizations and repositories (e.g. NISO 2004; Day 2005; van Ballegooie and Duff 2006).

2.5.1 Types of Metadata

For the purposes of this guide, metadata can be grouped loosely into a few categories (as described below). For the most part, these types of metadata are collected at a certain level (e.g. project or individual digital resource) but particular elements may be recorded for data from the general down to the specific file level. In addition, certain metadata standards may record elements of metadata that function for a number of purposes or levels as described below (e.g. 'Author' may aid resource discovery as well as provide technical or administrative information).

Project-Level Metadata is recorded at a broad level for an entire project/archive irrespective of the techniques used and covers elements such as period terms or dates, site and artifact keywords, project details, site codes and geographic location. Often, much of this information is included within documents in the archive (e.g., site reports).

Resource-Level Metadata is designed to allow the comprehensive description and easy retrieval of data sets, documents, and other digital objects. Many archives, including the US-based tDAR archive, distinguish a middle tier of metadata elements relevant to the individual resources that make up an archival project. A resource, by this definition, may include one or multiple files, depending on the context. A simple example might be a collection of PDF documents, images, or Access databases. A more complex example might be sensory data scans or GIS Shapefiles.

The purpose of this metadata largely overlaps with the project level, with a descriptive or research discovery emphasis, but focuses on details that may vary among resources within the context of a larger project, e.g., bibliographic citation fields, dates, locations, material types, or keyword-list elements that do not crosscut all resources in a project.

File-Level Metadata is typically very specific and relates to individual files. File-level metadata incorporates 'Technical' and 'Preservation' information describing the hardware and software used to create or modify the file along with validation methods such as checksums. In many cases, if the data are to be deposited in a digital archive, it is the archive itself that will generate much of this metadata. However, the data creator may have to record a number of elements, often during the process of data creation. Technical metadata is specific to data type and will therefore be covered within the later sections on specific data types.

A final broad category, **Administrative Metadata**, exists within all of the above and covers elements such as creation and acquisition, alteration, version control (Higgins 2006) and intellectual property rights. Such information can be recorded at a general level (e.g., ownership for an entire project archive may be held by one person or organization) but should also be recorded for a specific technique or case where personnel or authors and intellectual property right holders differ.

In addition to the benefits of a structured schema, metadata at any level can be further enhanced through the use of controlled vocabulary or standardized word list, e.g., the English Heritage *Monument Type Thesaurus* (English Heritage n.d.) and the controlled vocabulary for certain metadata fields in tDAR. Such standards may increase the usability and reliability of the metadata.

2.5.2 Project and Resource Level Metadata

General Project or Resource level metadata, like a good library catalogue, allows users to quickly and easily identify and evaluate the kind of information available in digital resources. This helps users to select the digital resources they are seeking. However, for this process to work effectively, the metadata has to be implemented accurately and clearly in a standard format. A commonly used format for descriptive metadata is Dublin Core (DCMI Usage Board 2012). The standard consists of fifteen kinds of information that provide an overview describing the project and includes information about geographical coverage, temporal dates, methodology, monument and evidence types. Within tDAR, the basic Dublin Core metadata schema has been extended to include a few additional archaeology-specific fields, as well as fields from the bibliographic Metadata Object Description Schema (MODS) standard (Library of Congress 2012b).

At the early stages of a project, metadata often cannot be accurately compiled; however, project workers should familiarize themselves with the types of generic project-level metadata required. When depositing data with an archive, the depositor often will need to complete a project- or resource-level metadata record form, together with any relevant format-specific (e.g., geophysical survey) templates.

The example below (Table 2.1) forms the foundation of ADS project-level metadata and consists of the basic Dublin Core elements. In tDAR this set of metadata elements corresponds to information collected at both the overall project level and, in many cases, for the individual resources (e.g., "project title" loosely corresponds to a more general "title" that may be used for individual documents or data sets at the resource level). It is also worth noting that tDAR metadata entry forms expand on this list to capture a variety of details that are grouped below (Table 2.2). More information on tDAR metadata is available in the tDAR Data Dictionary (tDAR 2011).

Table 2.1: ADS Project Metadata

Element	Description
Project Title	The title (and any alternatives) for the project.
Description	A brief summary of the main aims and objectives of the research project (or alternative process) from which the data collection arose together with a brief summary description of the content of the data.
Subject	Keywords for the subject content of the data (qualified using e.g., the English Heritage NMR Monument Type Thesaurus or the MDA Object Type Thesaurus.
Coverage	This is both spatial and temporal coverage. For spatial coverage it should include the current and contemporary name(s) of the country, region, county, town or village covered by the data collection and, where possible, a standardized reference such as the Getty Thesaurus of Geographic Names should be used (Getty Research Institute n.d.). If names or administrative units were different during the time period covered by the data they should be recorded separately. Site coordinates can also be entered as a National Grid reference in a number of different ways e.g., as a point (useful to describe a small project area via a central coordinate); as a line (e.g., at least 2 coordinates to represent the linear limits of the site); as a polygon (for a more complex site area, 3 or more coordinates are used to describe the boundaries). If applicable, the full postal code for the site can be included. For temporal coverage it should include the dates/period covered by the data (using existing thesauri where possible).
Creators	Details of the creator(s), compiler(s), funding agencies, or other bodies or people intellectually responsible for the data collection. Information should include forename, surname, affiliation, address, phone, fax, email, or URL.
Publisher	Details about any organization that has published this data.
Contributors	Other individuals or organizations who have contributed to the resource.
Identifiers	Project or reference numbers used to identify the data.
Source	Any important earlier work(s) from which this resource is derived.
Dates	Dates indicating when the data was created, when the archaeological project was carried out, processing dates, or computerization dates as appropriate.
Copyright	The name of the copyright holder for the data. If the collection was created during work by an employee, the copyright holder will normally be the employer. If the material is covered by a specific copyright (e.g., Crown copyright) please indicate this.
Relations	If the data collection was derived in whole or in part from published or unpublished sources, whether printed or machine-readable, this element should include references to the original material, details of where the sources are held and how they are identified there (e.g., by accession number). If the collection is derived from other sources, include an indication of whether the data represents a complete or partial transcription/copy and the methodology used for its digitization. Also include full references to any publications about or based upon the data collection.
Language	Indication of which language(s) the data is in (e.g. English, French, Spanish).
Resource Type	Whether the data is best described as primary data, processed data, an interpretation of data, or a final report.
Format	The format the data is saved in (e.g. WordPerfect 5.1, HTML, AutoCAD).

Completed examples of this type of schema can be found in Part 2.3 of the Archaeology Data Service *Guidelines for Depositors* (2012c).

Table 2.2: tDAR General Metadata

Element	Description
Basic Information	Basic metadata include association of a resource with a larger project, lifecycle status (e.g., draft, active, deleted), Language, Year Created, Abstract/Description and Physical Storage Location.
Bibliographic Metadata	Specific to documents, uses MODS metadata fields to describe resources.
Role(s) of Individuals or Institutions	These fields are used to credit individuals and institutions properly for their contribution to the resource. 'Role' refers to the individual's main role for the resource (e.g., creator, editor, etc.).
Resource Specific or Agency Identifiers	Describes agency or project identifiers used (e.g., Agency project number or Contract Number).
Investigation Type(s)	Lists all investigation types relevant to the resource (e.g., Research Design, Site Monitoring, Data Recovery/Excavation).
Site Description Information	Includes Site Name or numerical designation , Site Type (controlled vocabulary), and keywords
Material Type(s)	Artifact types covered by the resource (e.g., Ceramic, Fauna, Metal, Dating Sample).
Cultural Term(s)	Includes Culture (e.g., PaleoIndian, Archaic) and user-created values.
Temporal Coverage	Includes Temporal Terms (e.g., Pueblo IV), Coverage Dates, Date Type (e.g., Calendar, Radiocarbon), Start/End Years and Description (e.g., Calibrated, Range of ± N years).
General Keyword(s)	User-created values to describe aspects of the resource not covered by other metadata.
Spatial Terms	Includes Geographic Terms (e.g., Death Valley), Coordinates
Resource Provider	The institution that authorized the resource to be archived and disseminated.
Individual and Institutional Roles	Name, Current Email Address, Institution and Role of those involved with the resource.

2.5.3 File-Level Metadata

File-level metadata is information that allows an archive and users to understand the nature of the files within a project and their reuse potential. File-level metadata is highly dependent on the type of data being recorded and the file type itself, but commonly includes notes on elements such as the software used in creating the file, lists of file names, relationships between files and so on.

Although the first edition of the ADS *Digital Archives from Excavation and Fieldwork: Guide to Good Practice* recommended that each file in a digital archive should have an associated metadata record, experience has demonstrated that this level of documentation is largely unnecessary. Dependent on the nature of the data, groups of files of the same format or sharing other characteristics can be documented by a single metadata record. It was recognized that the provision of file-level documentation places a large burden upon the creator and substantially increases the time – and hence the cost – necessary to construct the archive. Research has also shown that users of digital data are more likely to search for entire archaeological projects, or for particular categories of information, reducing the need for individual file metadata.

Alternately, the US-based tDAR metadata schema recognizes that, for many kinds of records or resources that may be archived from an archaeological research project, it is worth the additional effort to maintain resource-level metadata records. For example, documents (e.g., site reports) or data sets generated from artifact-based analyses are well served by metadata records tied to each individual resource. But, at the same time, it may not be necessary to maintain separate metadata for every file – for example, cases where two versions of a document (one complete for archival and research purposes, another redacted to protect confidential information, such as specific site locations, from unauthorized viewers), essentially the same resource, are stored in the digital archive. Also, some file types, such as images, are more efficiently handled with primarily project-level metadata, similar to that advocated by ADS. File-level metadata is essential for discerning exactly what is in a file or group of files and how it can be used. It is recommended that, where data-specific guidelines do not exist, the following elements (Table 2.3) be recorded as a minimum standard at a file level.

Table 2.3: Basic file-level metadata

Element	Description
File Name	The name of the file e.g., report.doc
File Format	The file format e.g., PDF/A or Open Office Document
Software Used to Create the Files	The software used to create the file e.g., Microsoft Word 2007
Hardware Used to Create the Files	The hardware used to create the file; this is more significant when files are created directly by survey equipment such as laser scanners or GPS devices.
Operating System Used to Create the Files	The operating system under which the file was made e.g., Windows XP or Mac OS X 10.5.
Date of Creation/Last File Update	When the file was made or updated.
Processing History or Lineage	This element should be used to highlight relationships between files and whether a file is a source file or derived from another.

Technical metadata (Table 2.4) is used to plan future migration and validation strategies for the data. This metadata often includes a checksum that verifies whether a file has changed since the measurement was taken. The schema below is an example of the kinds of information about technical details that should be used for file-level metadata.

Table 2.4: Basic file-level technical metadata

Element	Description
Unique ID	Auto-generated unique ID e.g.,1234567
File Location	The file path i.e. directory and filename e.g. /adsdata/cottam_ba/jpg/fwking_plan.jpg
Checksum Type	The checksum algorithm used e.g., MD5, SHA-1, etc.
Checksum Value	The checksum value generated by algorithm e.g. 578cbb18f73a885988426797bcab8770
Project Id	A unique project ID e.g., ADS-123
Date Generated	Date the checksum was created e.g. 16-May-2006
Generated By	Person who created the checksum e.g. Doe, J
Last Audited	The date at which the file was last checked or verified e.g. 16-May-2007

In addition, an archive or data creator will want to maintain a process history of major tasks performed on files as part of archival practice. Again, this can be recorded as a simple text file. The following example (Table 2.5) is based on former AHDS practice.

Table 2.5: File-level process metadata

Element	Description
Process ID	Auto-generated unique ID e.g.,1234567
Project Id	A unique project ID e.g., ADS-123
Source Format	The format of the original file e.g., .txt
Destination Format	The destination format e.g., .shp
Process Agent	Who did the processing e.g., Doe, J.
Process Comments	Comments relating to the process undertaken e.g., 'referenced to WGS84'.
Process Start Date	Date that the process started e.g., 17-May-2007
Process Completion Date	Date process completed e.g., 17-May-2007
Process Description	A description of the process e.g., 'Import of XYZ data into ArcView for analytical purposes and dissemination as research outcome'.
Process Guidelines	Any guidelines related to the process.
Process Hardware Used	Hardware used to process the file e.g., Viglen Genie Intel Pentium 4
Process Software Used	Software used to process the file e.g., ESRI Arcview 9.1
Process Input	Full file path of the source file e.g., /adsdata/pro-453/xyz/file.xyz
Process Output	Full file path of the output file e.g., /adsdata/pro-453/shp/file.shp
Process Result	Comments on the result of the processing e.g., 'Success'.
Process Type	Description of the process carried out e.g., 'Conversion – dissemination'.

2.6 COPYRIGHT AND INTELLECTUAL PROPERTY RIGHTS (IPR)

2.6.1 General Topics

Copyright and intellectual property rights (IPR) are important considerations when planning for the digital archive throughout the life cycle of an archaeological project. The ease of dissemination and reuse of digital data makes copyright issues and other intellectual property rights particularly important to both creators and users of data. Both should be aware that copyright and IPR could exist automatically in any original work. Copyright and IPR laws differ significantly from country to country and these guides are intended to provide an overview of the issues involved but specific questions and issues may need further research. In general, it is important to ensure that rights are determined and/or resolved prior to contribution to an archive.

This section contains an overview of the issues related to copyright in the US and UK in general whereas subsequent sections cover country-specific issues.

Who Holds the Copyright

Commonly, the creator of the work or her/his employer holds the copyright of a work unless this has been formally transferred to another person or organization. This does not preclude contracts or funding sources from requiring that another party hold the copyright to a work that they have funded.

Recommendations and Related Considerations

In practice, archaeologists should negotiate with clients for whom they perform investigations to ensure that the data and documents created by their investigations are widely accessible and available. Archaeologists should ensure that contracts explicitly address copyright issues and make it clear in advance what information will be considered confidential when a project is complete. At the time when the information is deposited in an archive, it is important to identify any copyright holder(s). Also, if there are data, documents, or parts of documents in the archive that have restricted access, it is important to identify which individuals are allowed access to the digital archive and under what conditions.

In general, it is recommended that archaeological information held in digital archives be made available to the widest number of people possible. Metadata that provides summary information about what is contained in digital documents, images, data sets, etc. should be public so that, even if the digital resources themselves are confidential and not generally accessible, their existence will be known and interested researchers will be able to contact creators directly to attempt to obtain access to the digital resource. In the case of certain materials, there may be, however, temporary embargoes placed on information for a fixed period of time. In the case of confidential information, public agencies may restrict distribution of this information in order to ensure site protection. Data creators should also be aware of any responsibilities they may have under any relevant data protection or freedom of information legislation.

Raw Data

Raw data may have copyright restrictions and/or specific limitations of access or use. Restrictions and copyright will depend on the country in which it was produced. Regardless of the country-specific regulations, projects where data are digitized and/or digitized raw data are used, it is key that permission is sought and that sources are sufficiently documented within the project.

Licensed Materials

Certain materials, such as background or contextual geospatial survey data, are often acquired from sources external to a project and therefore owned by third parties who may retain a license to the information. In the majority of cases an external organization cannot archive such data without the express permission of the license holder and where commercial value still exists for the licensed data such permission is often unlikely to be granted. In such cases a potential solution is the creation of a 'distributed archive', i.e. one where the repository or archiving organization hold the derived data but also hold metadata that points to relevant raw data at the third party organization. Particularly in the case of sensory scans, GIS, and other complex data sources, such a distributed arrangement additionally has the advantage that maintenance and access to the large data set is maintained by a specialist organization other than the archive. The reverse of this, however, is that users who require access to the full data set may be required to purchase the raw data from the third party.

Metadata and Copyright

A key component to ensuring that rights are observed and maintained within an archive is their documentation. The relationships between records and individuals or organizations are key elements to record. It is essential that rights, use, and access conditions are clearly documented alongside names of the relevant data creators or licensees. As mentioned previously, where materials are digitized or purchased then such information should be recorded alongside details on how the data can be used.

Multimedia

It should be noted that these guidelines do not include an overview regarding copyright or intellectual property for moving image and sound files. Audiovisual and multimedia items have complex copyright protection. This is especially true of films, which can include a video of an excavation or a lecture, and in such cases there may be separate copyright protection for the moving images, sound track, screenplay and so on (e.g. US Code Title 17, ch. 10).

Other Considerations

Independent of copyright, the creators or contributors to intellectual property may have a moral right to be credited for their contributions to the work. It is important that such rights are clearly described and documented from the outset (e.g. consent forms for oral histories). In archaeology this right might extend to individuals making an important contribution within a large excavation team, or laboratory analysis. While it may not be possible to identify these people individually, it is consistent with ethical practice that their contribution be acknowledged. In most instances, this does not affect copyright.

2.6.2 Copyright in the UK

Generally, the creator of the work or her/his employer will hold copyright unless this has been formally transferred to another person or organization. This may not always apply to an archaeological project, and much will depend on the original source of funding. In projects where data are digitized, however, it is key that permission is sought and that sources are sufficiently documented within the project. Issues that should be considered when undertaking a digitization project are covered in the JISC Digital Media document *Learning Lessons from Other Digitisation Projects* (JISC Digital Media 2012a).

Data Creation and Copyright

In the UK the legal framework for copyright is provided by the 1988 Copyright, Designs and Patents Act. This act provides details of special Crown Copyright that exists on works made by the UK's sovereign or by a servant of the Crown (including employees of government agencies) in the course of duties.

The European Commission also has a variety of copyright directives that have been, or are being, adopted into UK law. These include copyright protection for the life of the creator plus 70 years (Directive 2006/116/EC) and copyright protection for databases (EEC 1996).

For current information on copyright in the UK, readers are directed to the following JISC Legal documents:

- Copyright Law Essentials (JISC Legal 2011a).
- Intellectual Property Law Essentials (JISC Legal 2011b).
- e-Repositories and the Law Essentials (JISC Legal 2007).

Copyright and Multimedia (Audio, Video, etc.)

The JISC Digital Media website provides a detailed overview of the issues associated with digital video and audio file in the document *Copyright and Other Rights for Creating Time-based Media Resources* (JISC Digital Media 2012b).

2.6.3 Copyright in the United States

In the United States (US) copyright is often held by the creator of a work or by the employer of the creator. However, some archaeological data and documents may not be restricted by copyright. This applies when archaeological data or documents are in 'the public domain'. Works are in the public domain if the copyright to the work has expired or been abandoned, or if the data or document is a US government work product (see below for more details on public domain). This is the case, when the work has been contracted by a US government agency or is conducted by US agency staff (US regulations call the products of such investigations 'US Government Work'). Examples would include archaeological studies contracted for by federal government agencies, such as, the US Forest Service or the Army Corps of Engineers, or investigations conducted by National Park Service archaeologists.

Data Creation and Copyright

In US law, copyright protection exists for the creators of original works of authorship fixed in any tangible medium of expression (17 USC. § 102(a)) or for the organization for which these individuals worked while they created the work ('Works Made for Hire', US Copyright Office (2010)). In specific instances, copyrighted works can be utilized under the Copyright Code policy of Fair Use. For more information on Fair Use, see the section entitled 'Fair Use' below or refer to the US Copyright webpage.

Creative works may be literary (non-fiction, fiction, or poetry) musical, dramatic, images, audiovisual, sound recordings, architectural works, or other kinds of tangible creative expressions. When considering issues of copyright, it's important to remember the law's constitutional purpose: to promote science and the useful arts. Copyright in the US was not intended to restrict the dissemination of knowledge through limitation of access or otherwise. A copyright is a right of intellectual property, whereby authors obtain, for a limited time, certain exclusive rights to their works. In the US, copyright is federal law derived from the 'copyright clause' of the US Constitution (Article 1, section 8, clause 8), which provides Congress with the power 'to promote science and the useful arts, by securing for limited times to authors ... the exclusive right to their ... writings'.

Limitations to Copyright

Not all works can be copyrighted, for example, as mentioned above, some works created by or for the US Government. Copyright protects only an author's original expression. It does not extend to any ideas, systems, or factual information that are conveyed in a copyrighted work, and copyright doesn't extend to any pre-existing material that the author has incorporated into a work (17 USC. §§ 102(b), 103). To be copyrighted, a work must be original; however, there is no requirement that the work be different from everything that has come before. The work need only embody a minimum level of creativity and owe its origin to the author claiming copyright.

Five Rights of US Copyright

In the United States, copyright holders have five basic rights:

1. The right to reproduce the work in copies.
2. The right to produce derivative works based on the copyrighted work.
3. The right to distribute copies of the work.
4. The right to perform the copyrighted work publicly.
5. The right to display the copyrighted work publicly.

Not all of these rights apply to all types of works.

The 'Fair Use' Doctrine

One of the rights afforded to the owner of US copyright is the right to reproduce or to authorize others to reproduce the work. This right is subject to certain limitations found in sections 107 through 118 of the copyright law (title 17, US Code). One of the more important limitations is the doctrine of 'Fair Use'. This concept allows users of a creator's work leeway in making use of the creative work without explicit permission of the creator.

The doctrine of Fair Use developed through a substantial number of past court decisions and is outlined in Section 107 of the Copyright Law. Section 107 contains a list of the various purposes for which the reproduction of a particular work may be considered fair, such as: criticism, comment, news reporting, teaching, scholarship, and research. Section 107 also sets out four factors to be considered in determining whether or not a particular use is fair:

1. The purpose and character of the use, including whether such use is of commercial nature or is for non-profit educational purposes.
2. The nature of the copyrighted work.
3. The amount and substantiality of the portion used in relation to the copyrighted work as a whole.
4. The effect of the use upon the potential market for, or value of, the copyrighted work.

The distinction between Fair Use and infringement may be unclear and not easily defined. There is no specific number of words, lines, or notes that may safely be taken without permission (US Copyright Office 2009).

Public Domain

A work in the 'public domain' is one that can be used by anyone for any purpose. Many documents, images, data sets, and other digital files created for archaeological studies are likely to fit within this category. There are guidelines for determining if a work can be considered part of the public domain, which can be summarized as follows:

- The copyright has expired.
- The work is a work of the US Government; such works can't be copyrighted (e.g. the results of archaeological investigations conducted by, contracted for, or required by a public agency).
- The work might be one that can't be copyrighted (e.g. titles, names, short phrases and slogans).
- The copyright might have been forfeited (e.g. the work may have been published without notice prior to the change in the law that eliminated the notice requirement (March 1, 1989).
- The copyright might have been abandoned, but this requires that the copyright holder intended to abandon the copyright and also generally requires an unambiguous statement or overt act on the part of the copyright holder that indicates his or her intent to dedicate the work to the Public Domain.

Most archaeological investigations conducted in the US are required to comply with federal laws that are intended to prevent the unmitigated destruction of significant archaeological resources. Many of these archaeological projects produce reports, data sets, images, and other digital files that are considered federal government works and are in the public domain. However, even for public domain works, federal agencies may restrict the distribution of 'confidential information', that is, information about specific archaeological site locations, the general release of which may cause 'adverse harm' to archaeological resources (e.g. maps showing sensitive site locations). While the bulk of a federal agency archaeological report may be in the public domain, an agency may redact confidential information and restrict access to it.

In general, it is US government policy to make available the results of research that have been conducted, contracted, or acquired by federal and other public agencies (Open Government Initiative 2012).

Part 3. Common Digital Objects

3.1 INTRODUCTION

The following sections provide an overview of commonly used file types that are generated by most archaeological projects. These types of files are typically created as part of standard archaeological investigations, including archival and collections research, fieldwork, and post-fieldwork processes. Recommendations are made about how these digital files should be archived.

These sections deal with basic and general file types for documents and texts, databases and spreadsheets, and images. Information on more specific file types associated with GIS, object scans, and remote sensing, can be found in the technique-based chapters featured in the online *Guides to Good Practice.*

In this section readers will find general guidance and more detailed and technical information about how specific file types are treated when they are deposited with digital repositories for long-term preservation. The general guidance and recommendations will be of most interest and use for project managers as they plan and undertake projects. The more specific information will be most useful for project personnel who are preparing files for ultimate deposit to the digital archive or repository where they will be preserved.

3.1.1 Issues to be Considered in Selecting File Formats and Saving Files

Numerous 'physical' obstacles may prevent future access and reuse of files (e.g. the deterioration or obsolescence of hardware and storage media). In addition, software obsolescence, caused by alternative or updated versions of software being released, resulting in the original software used to create and view the data becoming no longer available, must be considered. In such scenarios where proprietary formats are used, it may be impossible to access the original files without the hardware or software. Alternatively, where copies of the original software can be obtained, it may fail to run on modern machines. Examples of this problem include software like WordStar, and the proliferation of CAD or 3-D scan formats.

Choosing File Formats

When creating files it is important to consider how the choice of software will influence the sustainability of the files produced. Based on the issues described in section 2.1.1, data creators should choose applications that support file formats that are:

- common and in widespread use (i.e. *de facto* standards).
- independent to the software application (i.e. non-proprietary formats).
- where possible, openly documented and for which the specification is publicly – preferably freely – available.
- easily identified (e.g. not hidden by wrapper formats or compression techniques). Formats that have the ability to hold metadata within the file format will also aid in a format's identification and interpretation.

The Digital Preservation Coalition Technology Watch Report *File Formats for Preservation* (Todd 2009) discusses in detail the key issues involved in selecting suitable file formats for preservation.

The remaining parts of this section outline different file types and offer recommendations on formats.

3.2 DOCUMENTS AND TEXTS

Document and text files are arguably the most common file type created by archaeological research. Regardless of the type of work being undertaken, the majority of projects will produce various kinds of documents, including a final report. Documents consist predominantly of structured text (sentences, paragraphs, pages, chapters) but often include other elements such as images, figures and tabular data.

The digitization of documents and texts from paper or microfiche for the preservation or dissemination of pre-digital materials is also a large source of digital files. This process generally starts with a digitized image of each page, which may then be processed using optical character recognition (OCR) in order to make the final version of the document searchable, and possibly editable. The final text, which may also include images and figures, is predominantly stored using the PDF file format.

At present, digital documents and texts most commonly are created from scratch in word-processing packages such as Microsoft Word and OpenOffice. In the past, these types of files often were stored in proprietary binary file formats although more recent releases of both Microsoft Office and OpenOffice have highlighted a distinct move towards more archive-friendly xml-based formats and standards (e.g., DOCX, part of the Office Open XML format (ECMA-376) and ODT, part of the OpenDocument Format (ISO/IEC:26300:2006)). In addition to the formats in which documents are originally created, many text documents in their final versions may be stored and disseminated in a common publishing format, most notably Adobe's Portable Document Format (PDF), which allows the format and structure of a document to remain consistent across a variety of platforms while also removing much of the ability to edit.

Beyond common word-processing formats and PDF files, documents and texts may also exist in a range of plain text or marked up formats such HTML and XML.

Recommended Archival Formats for Preservation:

Many digital documents and texts remain in a single format throughout their lifecycle and many modern formats are suitable for preservation (Table 3.1).

Table 3.1: Recommended archival formats for documents and texts

Preservation Format	
.docx	Microsoft Office Open XML
.html/.xhtml	HTML or XHTML Document
.odt	Open Office Document Format
.pdf/a	PDF/A
.txt	Plain text document
.xml	XML Document

3.2.1 General Considerations

Document and text files are generally a component of a larger archive. While little project planning is required for the creation of a word-processed document, there are a few considerations that should be reviewed when it is expected that these files ultimately will be part of the digital archive of a project.

File Formats

There are two areas of concern regarding archival documents. The first of these is the continually developing nature of formats used by word-processing packages. Aside from the challenge of dealing with long-defunct software (e.g., WordStar), the continual development and enhancement of formats used by currently popular word-processing packages often results in incompatibility between older versions of a file and the current version of the software.

The adoption of XML-based open standard formats such as DOCX and ODT is an attempt both to standardize these formats and to allow different software packages to read non-native formats.

Considerations Regarding Embedded Objects in Documents

In addition to the file formats themselves, there are general concerns regarding embedded content within text documents and the implications this has for preserving such content in the long term within the original document format. The most common type of embedded content consists of images although in certain formats, most notably Microsoft Word and PDF, more complex content such as spreadsheets and video can be stored within the document itself. It is recommended that, in addition to archiving the document, images, spreadsheets, and other embedded content are stored and archived separately, thereby retaining the original qualities (e.g. image resolution or ability to manipulate data in a spreadsheet).

Other Considerations

Document creators should ensure that the content of a document is complete and self-explanatory. It is also important that, when saving the document to other formats e.g. for dissemination, the original is retained.

- Avoid including external links or dynamic content in documents, as these links may be lost or become unavailable over time.
- If intending to save the final version of a document to PDF, ensure that the original format (e.g. Word DOC, OpenOffice ODT, etc.) is retained separately, and archived.
- Additionally, if saving to PDF, ensure where possible that the file conforms to the PDF/A standard. This includes making sure that the file is not secured, includes no JavaScript, video or audio content or compression and that all fonts and images are correctly embedded and that the file is correctly 'tagged'.

3.2.2 Preparing Documents and Texts for Archiving

Before archiving a document, ensure the following:

- The version being archived is the final version of the document.
- If the document is a PDF, attempt to archive the final version of the source document as well. Also, ensure the PDF is saved as a PDF/A.
- Ensure that all of the embedded images, videos, or linked materials are also archived separately.

In deciding which formats are best to store your documents in for the long term, it is wise to consider one that both preserves the significant properties of the document and provides a format that can be readily accessed and, if necessary, can be migrated by various common applications.

Important Aspects of Documents for Preservation

A digital archivist when reviewing an archival process will evaluate whether the process preserves significant properties of a document. Generally, these properties represent the core components that preserve meaning. Significant properties of documents and texts that need to be preserved are:

- The words and order of the words in the document.
- The hierarchical structure of the document (e.g. different levels of headings).

- Formatting within the document (e.g. bold or italicized text).
- The page numbering of a document. This is particularly important where a document is a published or unpublished report or thesis. If users wish to cite and reference the document then retaining the correct text on the correct page is important (particularly so if files go through subsequent migrations).
- Any other non-text content such as images and data tables. Ideally this content is best stored separately.

The properties that are generally not seen as significant are:

- The font type and font size (unless this significantly changes pagination or formatting).
- Track changes functionality.

Significant properties may, however, change depending on the exact nature of the document being preserved. All files should be assessed on a case-by-case basis in order to determine which of the above are relevant.

Important Metadata for Documents and Texts

Although many documents are self-explanatory, it is recommended that for resource discovery basic metadata is recorded for each individual or set of related documents. There are a large number of long-standing metadata standards that have arisen from a wide variety of communities (e.g. Machine Readable Cataloguing (MARC) for libraries) and each has its strengths and weaknesses. Within the context of recording metadata for resource discovery (rather than technical file metadata recorded by formats such as textMD) the metadata set described below (Table 3.2) aims to record basic, general information about the document. This set of metadata is similar to other existing standards, most notably the fifteen elements of the Dublin Core Metadata Element Set (DCMI 2012). With documents in particular, there is a tendency for some overlap to exist between project level metadata and the metadata that describes documents produced as a result of a project (e.g. reports describing the project).

Table 3.2: Basic metadata for documents and texts

Element	Description
Title	Title of document.
Project Name	Name of associated project.
Abstract	Short description of the contents of the document.
Date Published	Year of publication.
Published	Where relevant, the full location details of any published versions i.e. series/journal title, issue and volume number. Start and end page numbers or number of pages should also be recorded.
Publisher	Name of document publisher and location.
ISBN	International Standard Book Number (ISBN)(where applicable).
DOI	Digital Object Identifier (DOI) (where applicable).
URL	URL (where applicable).
Related Files/ Resources	Details of related files or resources.
Language	The language (English, Spanish, etc.) used within the document. It is recommended that a controlled vocabulary (e.g. RFC 4646) is used and specified.
Author	Name of primary author(s).
Contributor	Names and roles of contributors, should be qualified e.g. Editor, Translator, Contributor.
Email	Email address for author.

In addition to the elements outlined above a number of other elements may need to be recorded at the document level (Table 3.3). These metadata categories provide additional descriptive information about the contents of documents.

Table 3.3: Additional metadata for documents and texts

Element	Description
Subject/ Archaeological Terms	Monument, site type, culture, object, material keywords.
Investigation Type	Type of investigation e.g. excavation, environmental sampling, etc.
Spatial Coverage	Single point or series of points defining site extents, minimum and maximum latitude and longitude.
Temporal Terms	Period keywords, start and end dates, radiocarbon dates.

3.2.3 Common File Formats and Archival Notes

In addition to these general considerations, each application and file format offers different benefits. Table 3.4 identifies the common formats used to create documents and texts along with their associated applications and their potential for use for long-term preservation.

Table 3.4: Common file formats for documents and texts

Extension	Notes
.DOCX	**This is an archival format** Part of the Office Open XML (OOXML) format created by Microsoft and an ECMA (ECMA-376) and ISO (ISO/IEC 29500-1:2008) standard. Released with Office 2007, Microsoft chose to develop their own specification (OOXML) rather than use the existing ODF international standard (ISO/IEC 26300:2006, see ODT below) in order to provide better backwards compatibility with earlier MS Word file formats. The format consists of human readable XML files packed with other content within a single zipped file. Embedded content should be stored separately.
.HTML .HTM .XHTML	**This is an archival format** Hypertext Markup Language (HTML) is a plain text-based markup language developed as a subset of SGML and maintained by the W3C. HTML is commonly used to create web pages. Aside from the plain text content of the HTML file (including either inline or linked stylesheets), websites generally consist of a wide range of linked media (images, video, audio, documents, etc.), which should be dealt with as separate objects. HTML is suitable for preservation and dissemination though documents must adhere to (and specify) a valid Document Type Definition (DTD) and character encoding. Where used, CSS styles should either be specified within the document or supplied as a separate file. Images and other media should be dealt with as individual objects as per other guidelines.
.ODT	**This is an archival format** Open Document Text (ODT) is part of the OpenDocument Format, an ISO standard (ISO/IEC 26300:2006) for XML-based office document formats. As an open XML-based format, ODT is suitable for preservation. As with the DOCX format, an ODT file is essentially a compressed zip file containing separate style, text (as XML) and embedded content (e.g. image) files. Files should be stored in their uncompressed form and, where the document contains images or other content, these should ideally be stored separately in a suitable preservation format.

Extension	Notes
.PDF/A	**This is an archival format** Based on the PDF format, PDF/A is aimed at providing a robust open-standard format for long-term archiving and is a published ISO standard (ISO 19005-1:2005). In order to provide a stable archive format, PDF/A requires that certain document elements (fonts and color spaces) are specified or embedded into the file while others (JavaScript, audio and video, encryption) are forbidden. The PDF/A format also has two levels of compliance; the basic level (PDF/A1-b) ensures that a document can be reliably visually reproduced while PDF/A1-a builds on this by including tagging/document structure. A useful overview of the PDF/A format is available (Bentley Historical Library 2009). PDF/A has been accepted as a viable format for long-term preservation and has been widely reviewed by the digital preservation community (e.g. Fanning 2008). However, as with standard PDF files, it is recommended that where files are created from another format (e.g. DOC or ODT) these are retained and deposited alongside the PDF/A file.
.RTF	**This is an archival format. Although, DOCX and ODT may be preferable.** Rich Text Format (RTF) is a tagged textual format developed by Microsoft. Although a largely human readable plain text format, and therefore suitable for both presentation and preservation, there are compatibility issues regarding formatting (e.g. textboxes and tables) when opening files in different word-processing packages. In addition, file size of an RTF file is generally much larger than the equivalent DOC, PDF or ODT file. Newer formats such as DOCX and ODT provide a more compact and compatible format and should be used in preference to RTF.
.SGML	**This is an archival format** Standardized Generalized Markup Language (SGML). A certified ISO standard (ISO 8879:1986 SGML) meta-language. SGML is used to define other markup languages such as HTML and XML.
.TXT	**This is an archival format** Simple plain text files are the 'lowest common denominator encoding for textual information' (Wynne and Yeates 2005: 2) and are widely compatible with a number of platforms and software. However, as a result, they support little in the way of formatting and can only be useful for the very simplest of documents. For all plain text files, an encoding (commonly US-ASCII or UNICODE) should be specified. Plain text files are covered in more detail in the AHDS Preservation Manual on Plain Text (Wynne and Yeates 2005).

Extension	Notes
.XML	**This is an archival format** Extensible Markup Language (XML) is a plain text based open standard produced by the W3C. XML was developed as a subset of SGML and is generally used on the web and for exchanging data between systems (e.g. databases). Suitable for preservation and dissemination though documents must adhere to (and specify) a valid DTD/schema and character encoding. Ensure that the xml documents include all dependent files, as the XML standard features the ability to include external files.
.DOC	**This is a commonly used, but not archival format. Check with your repository on whether it is accepted or needs conversion prior to submission. *DOCX, ODT, or PDF/A should be used instead.*** A popular format and the default for all versions of Microsoft Word from 1.0 through to 6.0, 95, and 97-2003. In addition to use within Word, DOC files can also be read in OpenOffice and can easily be converted to PDF. Compatibility between versions can be problematic. From 2008 the specifications for a number of Microsoft binary file formats were made available from the Microsoft website.
.PDF	**This is a commonly used, but not archival format. Check with your repository on whether it is accepted or needs conversion prior to submission. *DOCX, ODT, or PDF/A should be used instead.*** Many versions of PDF are NOT archival formats; ensure you use the PDF/A variant. PDF (Portable Document Format), created by Adobe, is primarily an open standard exchange format and has evolved many times since its creation with a number of variations, most notably PDF/A. PDF is aimed at cross-platform document exchange and, although a proprietary binary format, it is a highly suitable dissemination format as it retains document formatting and the reader is both free and widely available. In addition to standard text, PDF documents are also capable of storing embedded or linked media including raster and vector images, JavaScript and even 3-D data. In addition, PDF files may be secured in order to limit further editing or printing. A report, *'Preserving the Data Explosion: Using PDF'* (Fanning 2008), produced by the DPC highlights many of the issues involved in using PDF for preservation. In most cases a PDF file will be created from another format (e.g. DOC) and it is preferable to deposit and migrate from this original. Where this is not possible then a migration path to PDF/A is often the best route, though files should be checked to ensure that any embedded elements or security allow such a migration.
.SXW	**This is NOT an archival format. DOCX, ODT, or PDF/A should be used instead.** Part of the OpenOffice.org XML format used by OpenOffice/StarOffice from version 1.0 to version 2.0 and superseded by the OpenDocument Format Although this format has been superseded by ODT, it is structured similarly (i.e. zipped XML files) to ODT and can still be read by OpenOffice.org 2.0. Suitable for preservation but ODT should be used where possible.

Extension	Notes
.WPD	⊗ **This is NOT an archival format. DOCX, ODT, or PDF/A should be used instead.** A binary and proprietary format from WordPerfect. The popularity of WordPerfect has declined significantly since its initial release in the early 1980s in response to the rise of its main competitor, Microsoft Word. Although WPD (also WP or WP5 etc. for earlier versions) is the main format, more recent versions of the software support a wide range of import and export options.

In terms of lifecycles, for the most part document and text files remain in the same format while they are being created. An exception to this would be the PDF format in that few documents are created originally in PDF, the vast majority coming from a word-processed file (e.g. from Word or OpenOffice) that is then saved as a PDF document for dissemination.

3.3 DATABASES AND SPREADSHEETS

Both databases and spreadsheets are used to collect, organize, analyze, and store data. Databases can be more complex than spreadsheets, but a small database of a single table and a spreadsheet can be treated similarly. Databases and spreadsheets often provide both the framework and the substance of the data recovered by archaeological investigations. They are the raw material from which interpretations presented in reports about the project are based. They can also be the most useful source of information about any particular project when comparative analyses with data from other projects are undertaken. It is of great importance that metadata, including clear descriptive keys to any coding used, about the databases or spreadsheets is provided in the archive and carefully linked to the database and spreadsheet files.

This section provides general guidance for planning the inclusion of these kinds of files in a project digital archive. This is likely to be of most interest to project managers. Also described are issues regarding the specific and technical nature of digital archiving for these kinds of files, which will be of use for project staff creating the database and spreadsheet files that will be part of the digital archive. This guide does not aim to provide detailed guidance on the design of databases or spreadsheets beyond considerations that influence their preservation.

Functional Differences between Databases and Spreadsheets

Spreadsheets are simpler than databases in terms of structure and consist of single or multiple 'sheets' containing tabular data. Spreadsheets, however, contain not only the raw data itself but may also include formulas, graphs, charts, and images. They also allow for formatting of either cells or of the values within them. This formatting can be an important element of a spreadsheet and used to convey meaning or highlight specific elements. Data entry and use of a spreadsheet can be controlled to a limited degree through the use of protected or locked cells and cell-specific formatting (e.g. rounding values to limited decimal places or displaying them in currency formats). Some databases, such as FileMaker Pro, blur the lines between spreadsheets and databases by allowing formatting within any data value.

Databases build on the two-dimensional tabular structure of spreadsheets by enabling relationships among tables. In contrast to spreadsheets and many flat file databases, most database applications allow (and in fact require) the strict specification – in terms of field length, data type (numeric, etc.) of the data types to be recorded. The two most common database architectures are *Flat File* and *Relational* databases, although there is a slowly growing movement towards the use of *Object-oriented* database models. The flat file model is broadly similar to that of a spreadsheet, with all of the data packed into a single table. In flat file databases there can be an inherent looseness in the way that data is defined and recorded, along with a significant duplication of sets of information from record to record. The relational model addresses these and other issues by splitting related groups of attributes into separate tables that are then linked together through key fields (*Primary* or *Foreign* keys).

Some databases, such as Microsoft Access or FileMaker Pro, may contain additional elements including: forms, used for data entry or for running queries, and results or reports that result from user interaction both of which are considered as 'non-data' components of a database.

Regardless of their differences, spreadsheets and most databases are fundamentally tabular data, consisting of one or many sets of columns and rows.

Recommended Archival Formats for Preservation:

For the majority of databases and spreadsheets, the preferred format for preserving data is as ASCII-delimited text. However, it is important to check with your archive before choosing a format. Digital Antiquity, for example, has developed tools to accept and properly archive a wider range of formats including Access Databases, and older versions of Excel. Choosing the appropriate format will depend on properties of the database or the spreadsheet, such as formatting. Table 3.5 outlines the recommended archival formats for both databases and spreadsheets.

Table 3.5: Recommended archival formats for databases and spreadsheets

Preservation Format	
.csv	Comma separated values
.ods	Open Office Spreadsheet format
.tab	Tab separated values
.xlsx	Microsoft Office Open XML
.xml	XML Document

Other Formats

Portable Document Format (preferably PDF/A, see the section on Documents and Digital Texts) can occasionally be used to archive spreadsheet data in addition to another format. This should only be used where there is significant information present in the form of formatting and layout that cannot adequately be replicated in a CSV file and is lost when the data are migrated to an XML-based format (ODS or XLSX).

XML also offers a potentially reliable format for storing database data and a number of converters for a variety of database formats are currently available. One advantage of XML over simple delimited text formats is that a schema or Document Type Definition (DTD) can hold the data dictionary (i.e. information on the structure and format of the database) that cannot be so easily stored for delimited text files.

Another option for databases is the SIARD (Software Independent Archiving of Relational Databases) suite (Swiss Federal Archives n.d.). The SIARD Suite is based on a number of international standards (e.g. XML, SQL:1999 and UNICODE) and currently supports a variety of databases including Oracle, Microsoft SQL Server and Microsoft Access.

3.3.1 General Considerations

This section provides general pointers on ensuring that data in archived spreadsheets and databases is both consistent and easily reusable and remains so throughout its preservation lifecycle.

Avoid Embedded Objects

Many database and spreadsheet applications allow users to embed other media (especially images) within files. Whereas databases are more likely to store links to external files rather than the files themselves, spreadsheet applications such as Microsoft Excel and OpenOffice Calc allow users to embed graphs and charts generated from data along with other images. Again, as with document and text files, it is advisable that such content is stored and archived separately, thereby retaining the original qualities of the content (e.g. image resolution).

Ensure Data Consistency and Provide Documentation

Coded fields and data must be adequately described and documented. The documentation must be archived alongside the database or spreadsheet so that the meaning of fields or data is not lost over time. When uploading database or spreadsheet files to tDAR, contributors have the ability to attach coding sheets.

Avoid Dependency on Styles and Formatting

Spreadsheet applications in particular allow a great deal of formatting (i.e. font color and style, cell color, border styles) to be applied to data and the cells that contain it. Often, these styles can be used to convey meaning that can then be lost during data transformation, e.g., migration to plain text.

Other Considerations

Data creators should consider the following when creating databases and spreadsheets:

- Use controlled vocabularies, established word lists, and clearly described and defined keys for data description and entry.
- Assign columns and tables meaningful names (e.g., avoid 'table1' or 'Num' or 'UT', which may not be understandable in the future) and be aware that tables or sheets may not always remain packaged together within a single file.

3.3.2 Preparing Databases and Spreadsheets for Archiving

As far as many archives are concerned, the core of both a spreadsheet and a database are the data tables/worksheets themselves along with documentation and metadata describing the contents of and relationships between tables or sheets. The order or layout of the columns and rows may also be of significance (especially in spreadsheets where layout is significant) but forms, reports, queries and macros are not seen as core data and are therefore often not preserved.

Important Aspects of Databases or Spreadsheets for Preservation:

A digital archivist when reviewing an archival process will evaluate whether the process preserves significant properties of a data set. Generally, these properties represent the core components that preserve meaning. The significant properties of a data set – i.e. the most basic elements of a file that are to be preserved and maintained – are outlined below:

- **Data Values** – The actual data within the spreadsheet or database (there may be several sheets of data or tables) including cell headings and the values themselves.
- **Structure and Relationships** – Particularly with databases though also applicable to spreadsheets, it is important that the relationships between tables/sheets are documented and understood.
- **Graphics** – Any figures, graphs or charts in the database or spreadsheet.
- **Layout** – With spreadsheets in particular, where formatting and the use of color or certain styles is seen as adding meaning to the data, this meaning becomes a significant property and must be preserved in some way. This is commonly seen where spreadsheets are used as a means to lay out tabular data (which is often better done using word-processing software); in such cases alternative formats (e.g. PDF/A) should be used to preserve data, as such formatting is generally lost when exporting to plain text based formats.

General Checks

In addition to ensuring that the significant properties of a file are retained during any file conversions, there are certain checks to be made before a conversion can be carried out. These checks ensure that certain significant characteristics of a spreadsheet or database are not lost during the conversion process.

- **Data** – Check row counts after export and text for truncation – check field lengths (especially for databases); where the length of the data is the same as the field length it may indicate truncated values.
- **Special Characters and Delimiters** – Databases and spreadsheets can contain special characters or common delimiters (e.g. tabs or pipes) within the data set. Delimiters such as pipes, commas or tabs can present a problem if the file is to be migrated to delimited text and such characters should be identified early on so that the migration strategy can account for them. In addition to delimiters, special or foreign characters such as ampersands, smart quotes or the em dash (—) may also interfere with the export and subsequent display of the data. Databases and spreadsheets may also contain foreign characters that will often not export to a basic text file unless a specific character set (e.g. UTF-8) is specified.
- **Tables and Sheets** – Although the assumption is that databases or spreadsheets should be migrated in their entirety, an assessment of each part should be made as they may differ in structure or format. Spreadsheets contain a default number of blank worksheets when created and users often create additional sheets – or tables in databases – to store data temporarily that are not intended for preservation.
- **Formulae, Queries, Macros, and Views** – If the file contains complex formulae or queries that need to be preserved in their own right, then these need to be identified as migrated versions of the spreadsheet or database may only preserve the actual values calculated by the functions and not the functions themselves. Complicated formulae (e.g. those linking worksheets) or queries may need to be preserved separately and documented within a text file so the functionality can be recreated at a later date.
- **Comments or Notes** – As with macros and formulae, the migration process may not save comments or text notes added to a file. Before migration, comments will need to be stored in a separate text file with a clear indication of which file and cell the comment relates to.
- **Hidden or Protected Data** – Occasionally spreadsheets contain hidden or protected cells. These should be identified so that the migration strategy includes such data.
- **Links and External Data** – With databases in particular, it is important that the relationships between tables are understood, documented, and correct

(checks can be made to ensure that duplicate or orphan records aren't present). Worksheets within spreadsheets can also be linked through cells drawing on the values from other sheets, or external data lookups. Additionally, both databases and spreadsheets can link to (or hold the filenames of) files such as images that are held externally. If such external files are part of a project data set then checks should be made to ensure that these filenames are stored and archived correctly.

- **Layout and Formatting** – Layout and formatting, especially in spreadsheets, can be problematic in migrating data as these may be lost when migrating data to delimited text formats. Checks should be made for headings that span multiple rows or columns or information conveyed through use of color, borders or font. Depending on the nature of the formatting, either the data will need to be edited by hand before migration to ensure that meaning is not lost (e.g. with spreadsheets, merged cells must be split and the text within them duplicated within each cell) or an alternative migration format should be found, e.g. PDF/A.

File-naming

If files are to be preserved as delimited text then, for both databases and spreadsheets, the final data set will consist of a text file per table/worksheet. Where possible, files should retain the same name as the original (though the file extension may be different). Where multiple worksheets or database tables are being exported, filenames should reflect both the name of the original spreadsheet/database and the name of the worksheet or table that the data came from, for example:

[database name]-[table name].csv e.g. findsdatabase-lithics.*csv*

[spreadsheet name]-[worksheet name].csv e.g. siteregister-photos.*csv*

Where extra files are created to hold images, queries, notes or formulae, these should also be named in a logical way that makes it easy to trace exactly where they came from, for example:

[spreadsheet name]-[worksheet name]-[chart name].tif.

In some cases it may be necessary to change the table names to either shorten them or remove punctuation that cannot be used within a filename. In such cases it is important to remain as close to the original name as possible.

Although the relationships between files should be clear from the filenames, it is useful to store exported tables or worksheets together under a single directory. Any exported images or documentation can then be stored in sub-directories within this structure.

Additional Metadata for Databases and Spreadsheets

Databases and spreadsheets require metadata and documentation at a number of levels to ensure that they can be preserved and reused reliably. The following elements (Table 3.6) should be recorded and stored with the data set.

Table 3.6: General metadata for databases and spreadsheets

Element	Description
Project Title	Title of associated project
Name of Database/Spreadsheet File	Database or spreadsheet filename

In addition to the above, the following elements (Table 3.7) should be recorded for each worksheet/table within your spreadsheet/database.

Table 3.7: Worksheet/table specific metadata for databases and spreadsheets

Element	Description
Name of Worksheet/Table	Spreadsheet worksheet or database table name
Purpose of Worksheet/Table	Description of the worksheet/table
Number of Rows of Data	Total number of rows of data within the table
Primary Keys (Database Only)	Field names of any primary keys within the table
Foreign Keys (Database Only)	Field names of any foreign keys within the table

The elements described below in Table 3.8 should also be recorded for each column/field within your spreadsheet/database.

Table 3.8: Column/field specific metadata for databases and spreadsheets

Element	Description
Field Name	Name of database field or spreadsheet column.
Field Description	Full description of fields and codes or terminology used. Alternatively, codes used within a data set can be supplied as a separate document.
Data Type and Field Length (Database Only)	The data type (e.g. text or number) and field length (e.g. 255 characters)
Coding Sheet	(If needed in spreadsheet)

The elements above essentially make up the 'data dictionary' commonly associated with databases. In addition, for databases in particular, it is also necessary to describe the relationships between tables either in words or by the inclusion of an entity relationship diagram (Fig. 3.1).

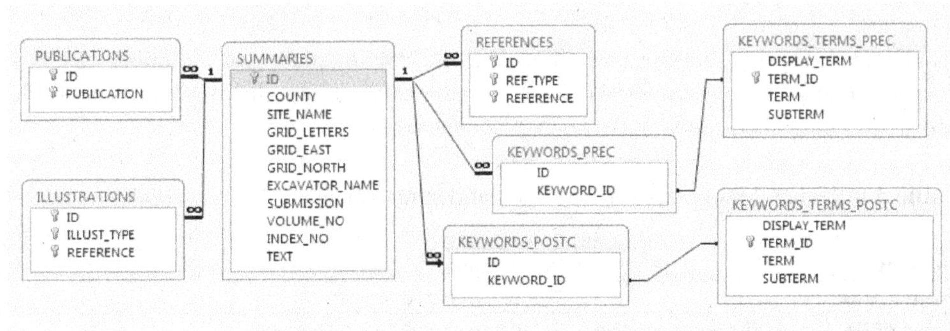

Figure 3.1: *Example entity relationship diagram*

Documentation can also include any extra features in the spreadsheet or database that require preservation, for example, formulae, queries, macros, and comments. These can generally be stored alongside the data as text files.

3.3.3 Common File Formats for Databases and Spreadsheets

The tables below outline some of the common formats used to create databases (Table 3.9) and spreadsheets (Table 3.10) and describe their associated applications and potential uses for long-term preservation. As with many word-processing applications, spreadsheets in particular have seen a move in recent years towards support for common XML-based file formats and it is worth noting that many applications such as Microsoft Office, OpenOffice and WordPerfect Office have support for both Office Open XML (OOXML) and OpenDocument Format (ODF) file formats.

How to use these tables:

Tables 3.9 and 3.10 describe common file formats for databases and spreadsheets as well as their archival equivalents. Each format includes the following:

- File Extension.
- Whether the format is considered 'archival'.
- If the format is not 'archival' what format it should be converted to for archiving.
- Notes on the format.

Databases

Table 3.9: Common file formats for databases

Extension	Notes
.CSV	**This is an archival format** Comma-separated values (CSV) is a plain text format (described by RFC-4180). Unfortunately, different programs have different support for the CSV format. Be careful when using this format to ensure that both commas and quotes are properly escaped. This format may not be appropriate for data that contains accented or special characters outside of the standard ASCII set (as there is no mechanism to specify charset). Be sure to include a first row that includes column names.
.TAB	**This is an archival format** Tab-separated values, an IANA Standard (Open Format). While open, this format may not be ideal for archiving as it does not support the use of tab-characters within values. This format may not be appropriate for data that contains accented or special characters outside of the standard ASCII set (as there is no mechanism to specify charset). Be sure to include a first row that includes column names.
.XML	**This is an archival format** Storing data in an XML representation can be useful as it better captures the structure and relationships of the data. However, there is no specific schema or structure for this data that is recognized as an interchange format. This format may be better than TAB or CSV in some cases, especially with more complex data sets or data that uses non-ASCII characters.
.ACCDB	**This is a commonly used, but not archival format. Check with your repository on whether it is accepted or needs conversion prior to submission. *TAB, CSV, or XML should be used instead.*** A proprietary Microsoft format first introduced in Access 2007 and continued with Access 2010 and developed in order to include enhanced functionality over the previous MDB format. The ACCDB format, as with previous MDB files, continues to be based on the Jet Database Engine. The ACCDB format is not recommended for long-term storage but Access does support output in a number of suitable alternative formats.

Extension	Notes
.DBF .DBT .NDX	✖ **This is NOT an archival format. TAB, CSV, or XML should be used instead.** Originally used by dBASE but also adopted by others (e.g. ESRI for ArcInfo) DBF has emerged as a generic format with a number of (often incompatible) variations, often referred to as 'xBase'. Although the file structure is simple and documented (Bachmann 2010), it is important to be aware of the specific software application used in creating the file. The format has potential for long-term storage but, due to variations on the standard, it is important to know exactly how the file has been created. dBase, as with most applications, supports output to more suitable formats.
.FM .FM3 .FM5 .FM7 .FM12	✖ **This is NOT an archival format. TAB, CSV, or XML should be used instead.** Used by FileMaker Pro, this format is closed and proprietary, and is only readable by the application. FileMaker Pro has a similar feature set to Microsoft Access. The format is not viable for long-term preservation or storage due its proprietary nature, though later versions do provide an XML export option that will ensure the appropriate capture of the data.
.MDB	? **This is a commonly used, but not archival format. Check with your repository on whether it is accepted or needs conversion prior to submission. *TAB, CSV, or XML should be used instead.*** A proprietary Microsoft format used by Access databases (2003 and earlier) and now replaced by the ACCDB format. In essence, the MDB format packages up the Access interface with the actual database engine (Jet Database Engine). Inevitably there have been updates to Jet (Access 2.0 uses version 2.5, Access 95 uses version 3.0, Access 97 uses version 3.5, Access 2000–2003 use version 4.0) with the result that there have been format changes to the MDB file. The MDB format is not recommended for preservation but Access supports output in a number of suitable formats.
.ODB	✖ **This is NOT an archival format. TAB, CSV, or XML should be used instead.** An XML-based database format used by OpenOffice Base. Like ODF formats, an ODB file consists of a series of zipped XML files where content is contained in a 'content' xml subdocument and additional subdocuments contain style information, document metadata, and application-specific settings. In addition, ODB – like Access formats – also consists of an interface (which can access external data sources) and a database engine (in this case, the HSQL database engine).The ODB format is not recommended for long-term storage but many of the applications that use this format (especially OpenOffice) support output in a number of suitable formats.

Extension	Notes
.SQL	**This is NOT an archival format. TAB, CSV, or XML should be used instead.** Used by relational databases like Oracle, PostgreSQL, MySQL, and Microsoft SQL. Although SQL is fairly common and has a number of standard formats, it is difficult to ensure that a SQL file is fully compliant with any of the standards. Most databases maintain their own variations of the SQL standard and thus it becomes difficult to maintain compliance.

Spreadsheets

Table 3.10: Common file formats for spreadsheets

Extension	Notes
.CSV	**This is an archival format** Comma-separated values (CSV) is a plain text format (described by RFC-4180). Unfortunately, different programs have different support for the CSV format. Be careful when using this format to ensure that both commas and quotes are properly escaped. This format may not be appropriate for data that contains accented or special characters outside of the standard ASCII set (as there is no mechanism to specify charset). Be sure to include a first row that includes column names.
.ODS	**This is an archival format** Part of the OpenDocument suite of formats, an ISO standard (ISO/IEC 26300: 2006) for XML-based office document formats. Primarily used by OpenOffice Calc (version 2.0 onwards). As with the OpenDocument Text (ODT) format, the ODS file is essentially a compressed zip file containing separate style, text (as XML) and embedded content (e.g. images) files. As an open XML-based format, ODS is suitable for long-term preservation though ideally the files should be stored in their uncompressed form. Additionally, where the document contains images or other content, these should ideally be stored separately in a suitable preservation format. As with all spreadsheet data, the ability to migrate to a plain text format should be considered for maximum accessibility.
.TAB	**This is an archival format** Tab-separated values is an IANA Standard (Open Format). While open, this format may not be ideal for archiving as it does not support the use of tab-characters within values. This format may not be appropriate for data that contains accented or special characters outside of the standard ASCII set (as there is no mechanism to specify charset). Be sure to include a first row that includes column names.

Extension	Notes
.XLSX	✔ **This is an archival format** Part of the Office Open XML (OOXML) format created by Microsoft and an ECMA and ISO standard. The format consists of human readable XML files packed with other content within a single zipped file. As a documented and open standard, XLSX is suitable for long-term preservation although embedded content should be stored separately. As the file is essentially a zipped archive it may also be best to store the content in an uncompressed format. As with all spreadsheet data, the ability to migrate to a plain text format should be considered for maximum accessibility.
.SXC	✖ **This is NOT an archival format. CSV, TAB, ODS, or XLSX should be used instead.** Part of the OpenOffice XML suite of formats and used by OpenOffice 1.0 Calc, the OpenOffice XML SXC format (now replaced by OpenDocument ODS) is, like its successor, an XML-based format. The format itself consists of a compressed XML file, with the actual spreadsheet data being stored in a file and images and other content in a separate directory. While an open and text-based format, it is recommended that the newer ODS is used in preference to SXC.
.WQ .QPW	✖ **This is NOT an archival format. CSV, TAB, ODS, or XLSX should be used instead.** A proprietary format used by the Quattro Pro spreadsheet application (now part of the WordPerfect Office Suite). Older files are also supported by Microsoft Excel 2000 (for Quattro Pro for Windows versions 1–5 the Quattro Pro Converter is available) but there can be problems importing these files into Excel e.g. graphs, embedded objects and macros in Quattro Pro for Windows are lost when the file is imported into Excel. Current versions of Quattro Pro support OOXML formats.
.XLS	? **This is a commonly used, but not archival format. Check with your repository on whether it is accepted or needs conversion prior to submission. *CSV, TAB, ODS, or XLSX should be used instead.*** A proprietary binary format used by Microsoft Excel (up to Excel 2003). Although a proprietary Microsoft format, the Excel XLS format is widely used and can be imported by a number of third-party applications (e.g. OpenOffice and Google Docs). The format has been replaced by the XML based formats (notably XLSX) in versions of Microsoft Office since 2003.

3.4 DIGITAL IMAGES

Digital images are used for a wide range of purposes, from data recording as photographs and drawings through to dissemination and interpretation as the output of CAD, GIS and virtual reality applications. In this section, digital images are discussed in two main sub-sections: raster images and vector images. As well as a difference in terms of file formats, the division into these two categories also reflects a fundamental difference in the type of data being created.

Types of Images: Raster and Vector

Raster images are most commonly photographs. Technically, they consist of an image composed of a matrix of pixels with a fixed size/resolution. Raster images can be created from a wide variety of processes ranging from original data capture such as digital photographs, scans and drawings through to outputs or 'products' such as plotted geophysical survey data and images from GIS layouts.

Vector graphics are most commonly drawings or plans and represent objects as geometric entities or vector objects rather than as an arranged grid; they have no fixed size or resolution. Vector objects can include lines, circles, rectangles and curves, all connected by points and paths. Vector graphics may contain two- or three-dimensional geometry and many files may also include layers containing raster data.

3.4.1 Raster Images in Archaeology

This section describes common types of raster image created as components of archaeological research, including:

- Digital photographs.
- Aerial photographs.
- Document scans.
- Screenshots and output from vector applications.
- Original images such as illustrations, posters, etc.

Recommended Archival Formats for Preservation:

The formats described in the table below (Table 3.11) are recommended for the long-term preservation of digital raster images:

Table 3.11: Recommended archival formats for raster images

Preservation Format	
.dng	Digital Negative Format
.tif/.tiff	TIFF 6.0 File (uncompressed)

Alternative files, mainly those using compression to reduce archive sizes, have been suggested and investigated recently (see Gillesse et al. 2008). There may be scope to use files such as PNG and JPEG2000 as archival formats but, as these employ compression, they are not recommended.

3.4.2 General Considerations

Raster image formats vary widely in individual features and capabilities. The range of individual features and capabilities each file format possesses include: compression (lossless or lossy), color depth, support for transparency, and embedded metadata. Changes to file format can result in loss of data or quality, so it is important that an appropriate file format is chosen during the data creation stage, for any modification, and for long-term storage.

Resolution

Resolution describes the level of detail within an image expressed as a pixel count (e.g. pixels per inch [ppi]). The higher the resolution, the more detail is captured in an image and, consequently, the larger the file size. Simple black and white text generally requires a lower resolution (300 dpi) than a full-color photograph (600 dpi or higher), detailed map, or negative (1200 dpi or higher) (Library of Congress 2011). You will need to experiment with different resolutions to ensure that appropriate detail is captured in any scan and it is important to balance the level of detail required from an image against the size of the files created. Reducing resolution will reduce the quality of the image; once this has been done, it is impossible to restore the lost data.

Bit Depth

In addition to the resolution of an image, bit depth (or color depth) refers to the level of color information used by each pixel. Images can range in bit depth from 2 bit (i.e. black and white) through to 8 bits (usually gray scale), and 24 bits (standard color). As with resolutions, it is important to consider the bit depth in relation to the image being created and choose one that captures the information required while also minimizing file size.

Color Space

Color space should be considered in addition to bit depth and is used to refer to the color system or model used in an image. A key distinction exists between the two main systems: RGB (Red, Green, Blue), which is used primarily in images destined for on-screen display and the CMYK (Cyan, Magenta, Yellow, Black), which is used in printing. The RGB system can hold more combinations of colors than the CMYK system so it is important to be aware that, when printing, RGB-based images may not print accurately.

Compression

Many image formats use compression to help manage the file size. Some compression models can be lossy, i.e. the process of compression will cause data to be lost – this may not be visible until multiple modifications have been made. A number of formats, such as TIFF and PNG, allow data to be stored without any compression. When creating data it is important to be aware of when compression is being used (e.g. within a camera when capturing a JPG image) and the level/quality at which this is happening. Image compression is covered in detail in *Digital Preservation Guidance Note 5: Image Compression* produced by The National Archives (UK) (Brown 2009).

Transparency

Image transparency, i.e. elements of an image that are transparent, is supported in most vector formats but in only a few raster formats (e.g. TIFF, PNG and GIF). Although a minor consideration, it is important to be aware that, where elements of an image have been made transparent (either through an alpha channel or a transparent color), such functionality may not be supported in other formats or other stages of a particular workflow.

Image Layering

The layering of components within an image is a common function of many popular graphics packages (e.g. Photoshop or Photo-Paint) but is not supported in many raster file formats (the layers are conflated or merged from the top down). It is important to be aware that, when saving to a raster format, such layering will likely be lost.

3.4.3 Preparing Raster Images for Archiving

Selecting which images to archive will depend on the project and subject matter of the investigation for which the archive is being created. Deciding upon the type of image files to archive will depend on the individual workflow of which the image is a part. General guidance is to archive, where possible, the original data in an uncompressed open format.

- Digital cameras often provide limited options in terms of the files that they will produce. With images from digital photography this may entail storing either the original JPG (preferably as an uncompressed TIFF) or raw file in DNG or TIFF format.
- Images from document scanners will normally require the user to select a format to save to once the image has been scanned. With scanned images it is recommended that, prior to any processing and regardless of the final intended format, files should be saved in an open uncompressed (or lossless) format such as TIFF.
- Images created in graphics packages will require the user to select a format to save to and most packages support a wide range of formats. With files output from software such as GIS or CAD, the choice of image file format can often be more limited. In such cases an uncompressed format is preferred but, where this is not an option, files may be converted in other packages to a suitable archive format.

Many files, and particularly digital photographs, contain metadata packaged within the file format that may be useful for file documentation and reuse. In most cases, where such metadata exists and is deemed useful, it is advisable to retain and archive it in a separate format (e.g. as a text file or within a database).

In many cases archiving digital images requires either saving directly, or converting to, a stable preservation format. Where composite images have been created in a graphics-editing package (e.g. Photoshop or Photo-Paint) there may be value in saving the individual components as separate archival files as well. Such a strategy can also be applied to simple animated image files such as GIFs, where each frame would be exported to a separate file in a preservation format.

Important aspects of images for preservation:

The significant properties of raster images related to their preservation are discussed in detail in the *Significant Properties Testing Report: Raster Images* (Montague 2009) but are outlined here below.

- **Image Size and Resolution** – conversions should ensure that the original resolution and image size remains the same in the preservation file format. In addition it is important that, when converting files to a new format, lossy compression is not applied to the image.
- **Bit depth** and **Color space** – converted files should ensure that the bit depth and color space of the original image are supported in preservation formats and that images are not degraded when converted.

Although these properties are components of all image formats, it is important to ensure that these properties remain the same or retain the same values when converting files to archival formats.

Additional Metadata for Raster Images

Metadata for raster images is discussed in detail in *Guidelines for Handling Image Metadata* (Metadata Working Group 2009) and on the JISC Digital Media (2012c) page discussing *Metadata and Digital Images*. Image metadata can cover a wide range of areas (structural, descriptive, administrative and technical metadata) and can be either embedded within the image file (e.g. in EXIF, IPTC and XMP) or stored as a separate file (database, spreadsheet or text document).

Embedded technical metadata, commonly in the EXIF format, generally describes the creation of the image file and records various camera settings used in capturing the image. There has been much discussion regarding whether automatically generated metadata such as EXIF should, or should not, be considered a significant property. There are obviously scenarios where such metadata is consciously used by a data creator and is inherently significant, but commonly this is not the case. There is also the potential that certain metadata elements (e.g. date), where not deliberately used and correctly set, can actually contain incorrect information. Embedded metadata within images has, however, become common practice and a decision should be made when converting or reproducing images regarding whether this metadata is valuable and should be retained. Generally, if embedded metadata is seen to be valuable, it should be preserved separately.

Other technical elements may be included in embedded metadata sets but are more commonly recorded as separate files (e.g. text files or spreadsheets) due to the varying requirements of each data creator and archive. Common technical metadata elements include documenting capture device information, software and editing history.

Tables 3.12 and 3.13 list suggested metadata elements and have been drawn together from various sources (Eadie 2005; Metadata Working Group 2009; DCMI Usage Board 2012). It is important to note that some of these elements can be applied to an entire collection (e.g. a set of photographs) and would not need to be repeated for each file.

Table 3.12: General metadata for raster images

Element	Description
Identifier	Image filename, e.g. survey01.tif
Title/Caption	The title of the image or a suitable caption
Description	Description of the image
Creator	Name of image creator
Date	Date on which image was created
Rights	Details of copyright or other rights and holder details
Keywords	Keywords e.g. period, site or feature terms. Use suitable thesauri where they exist
Location	Location information for the image. Where possible use a standardized format e.g. Latitude/Longitude or keywords from a suitable thesauri e.g. Getty Thesaurus of Geographic Names (Getty Research Institute n.d.)

Table 3.13: Technical metadata for raster images

Element	Description
File Format and Version	e.g. TIFF 6.0
File Size	Size of the file in bytes
Spatial Resolution	The resolution of the image measured in pixels per inch (ppi)
Dimensions	Dimensions of the image in pixels e.g. 400 x 700px
Color Space	The color space used in the image e.g. RGB or gray scale
Bit Depth	e.g. 24bit or 8bit
Capture Device	Either the camera make and model or details of the scanner
Capture Software	Software used to capture the image (generally used for scanned images) e.g. Adobe Photoshop CS3

When using embedded metadata, it may be best to duplicate this metadata externally as data or format migrations may affect such metadata (and in some cases cause data loss). For example, EXIF metadata is supported by JPEG and TIFF but not – at least in the same way – by JPEG2000 (LaBarca 2010) and PNG formats.

3.4.4 Common File Formats for Raster Images

The table below (Table 3.14) outlines many of the common raster image formats currently in use.

How to use this table:

Table 3.14 describes common file formats for raster images as well as their archival equivalents. Each format includes the following:

- File Extension.
- Whether the format is considered 'archival'.
- If the format is not 'archival' what format it should be converted to for archiving.
- Program or Standard associated with the file.
- Notes on the format.

Table 3.14: Common file formats for raster images

Extension	Notes
.DNG	**This is an archival format** Based on (and compliant with) the TIFF/EP format, Adobe Digital Negative (DNG) is an openly documented archival format for the storage of raw files generated by digital cameras. Adobe developed DNG in the hope that it will become a single raw processing solution that enables a more efficient workflow when handling raw files from multiple camera models and manufacturers (existing RAW image formats can be converted to DNG via the free Adobe DNG Converter available from Adobe's website). The DNG format is able to read all image tagging (EXIF and IPTC) from the original RAW file and store these in the DNG image and, in addition, supports other metadata to be embedded via the Extensible Metadata Platform (XMP). DNG is suitable for the long-term storage of image data.
.TIF **.TIFF**	**This is an archival format** Baseline TIFF 6.0 is a *de facto* standard and widely used in an uncompressed form for storing archival versions of images. The TIFF format is flexible and can support a number of options such as LZW compression (the Lempel-Ziv-Welch lossless data compression algorithm), multiple pages and metadata embedding, and data creators should be clear on what type they are producing. The TIFF format supports embedding of EXIF metadata as well as GeoTIFF metadata for georeferencing. Generally the uncompressed baseline 6.0 is seen as being the only suitable format for preservation although extensions such as GeoTIFF and TIFF/EP (both containing specialized metadata) are equally acceptable and based on this standard.

Extension	Notes
.BMP	**This is NOT an archival format. DNG or TIF should be used instead.** Commonly used in many older Windows applications, the BMP format is similar to GIF in that it is ideally suited for simple graphics. The format does optionally incorporate compression although this is not as efficient as that of GIF. BMP has limited options for embedding metadata. Not recommended as either a working format or a format for long-term storage.
.CPT	**This is NOT an archival format. DNG or TIF should be used instead.** Primarily used for creating or editing images. CPT is the native format of Corel Photo-Paint and, as the main competitor to Adobe Photoshop, provides a similarly wide range of functionality. As with the PSD format, CPT is ideally suited to the creation and editing of images and, while copies may be kept in this format for possible future editing, the format is highly specific to Corel software and copies of images should be stored in uncompressed formats such as TIFF.
.GIF	**This is NOT an archival format. DNG or TIF should be used instead.** Widely used on the Web for both still and animated images, the Graphics Interchange Format (GIF) offers lossless compression but with a limited palette (8 bit/256 colors) and limited options for embedding metadata. Although it has now been superseded by more up-to-date formats (e.g. PNG), the GIF format is still widely in use. It is recommended that either the PNG format is used if compression is required or TIFF for long-term storage.
.JP2 .JPX	**This is NOT an archival format. DNG or TIF should be used instead.** JPEG2000 is an ISO standard and an intended replacement for the JPG format. The uptake of JPEG2000 has been relatively slow since its release in December 2000 with browser support still lacking. The format offers higher performance and lossless compression ratios aimed at minimizing file size and compression artifacts. The format also differs from standard JPG in that it uses XML (the JPX format) to store metadata within the file and can include within this IPTC, GML and Dublin Core metadata elements (Joint Photographic Experts Group 2007). The format is now widely being investigated as a viable format for preservation due to its use of lossless compression and scalability. Various institutions and organizations such as the Wellcome Library (Buckley 2009), the University of Connecticut (Lowe and Bennett 2009) and the Digital Preservation Coalition (Buckley 2008) have produced reports in the last few years that suggest JPEG2000 will become increasingly popular as a preservation format.

Extension	Notes
.JPG **.JPEG**	**This is a commonly used, but not archival format. Check with your repository on whether it is accepted or needs conversion prior to submission. *DNG or TIF should be used instead.*** An ISO standard format developed by the Joint Photographic Expert Group. The JPG format was primarily designed for photographic or painted images with smooth varying tones. The format offers 32-bit color depth and extremely efficient lossy compression algorithms. JPEG also allows EXIF and IPTC metadata to be embedded within the file. Although JPG files are usually drastically smaller than their TIF or PNG equivalents, the use of lossy compression makes them unsuitable for long-term storage. Where compression is required, data creators are advised to use the JPEG2000 format with lossless compression.
.PNG	**This is a commonly used, but not archival format. Check with your repository on whether it is accepted or needs conversion prior to submission. *DNG or TIF should be used instead.*** Portable Network Graphics, an ISO standard and supported by the W3C. Intended as a replacement for the GIF format, PNG offers 32-bit color depth, lossless compression, support for an Alpha channel (transparency) among a host of other features. PNG does not, however, support standard EXIF metadata and, as the format was primarily designed for internet use, it does not support color spaces other than RGB. PNG has become the format of choice for lossless presentation. Although TIFF is the preferred format for long-term storage of images, PNG offers certain advantages over JPG (e.g. less visible artifacts) but it is still not recommended for use with digital photographs.
.PSD	**This is NOT an archival format. DNG or TIF should be used instead.** Adobe Photoshop document file is a proprietary format owned by Adobe. Primarily used for creating or editing images. The PSD format is highly flexible and is often touted as an 'industry standard' imaging solution. The format supports masks and layering, transparency, text and a number of other features making it an ideal format in which to create and edit images; it also supports EXIF, IPTC and XMP metadata. PSD has limited compression support and thus files tend to be large. The PSD format is an ideal format in which to create and edit files but its proprietary and closed nature means that there is limited third-party support and it is unsuitable for long-term storage. While copies of a file could be stored in the PSD format so that future editing (if desired) would be possible, migration of images to open uncompressed formats – i.e. TIFF – is advised for long-term accessibility.
RAW ***(various extensions)***	**This is NOT an archival format. DNG or TIF should be used instead.** Raw bitmap files are usually vendor specific and proprietary in nature. Raw files are unprocessed bitmap files in a number of different formats created directly by a digital camera (and occasionally by digital scanners). Due to the lack of standardization it is almost impossible to characterize a raw file; many files are uncompressed but other use both lossy or lossless compression (and some allow users to select). The lack of standardization also means that many files require specific software applications to open the files. Raw formats are unsuitable for long-term storage and data creators are advised to convert such files, where possible to standard formats such as TIFF or DNG.

3.4.5 Vector Images in Archaeology

The most common examples of vector images are 2-D images/illustrations, usually produced for publication purposes and often derived from CAD (e.g., archaeological feature or building illustrations) or GIS (e.g., site plans or distributions). Very frequently these images are incorporated into PDF files as part of a site or project report.

This section aims to cover simple 2-D vector images that are not part of a discrete technology such as CAD or GIS. Vector files created in these applications are covered in the online *Guides to Good Practice*. Vector images are also covered in great detail in the AHDS *Digital Images Archiving Study* (Anderson et al. 2006) and in the JISC Digital Media document *Introduction to the Vector Image Format* (JISC Digital Media 2012d).

Recommended Archival Formats for Preservation:

Table 3.15: Recommended archival formats for vector images

Preservation Format	
PDF/A	Adobe PDF variation A
SVG	Scalable Vector Graphic

3.4.6 General Considerations

This section covers images that have been created within a vector graphics package, or where a derived file (e.g. an illustration with added features such as descriptive text) is seen as being worth preserving in its own right. It is advised that if an image is derived from a CAD file or other format, then preservation of the original file should be preserved as well as the derived image. In many cases, derived vector images are frequently used for illustration purposes in documents such as project reports and so are also present elsewhere in a project.

3.4.7 Preparing Vector Images for Archiving

Vector images often are created in archaeology as a step within a larger project workflow; it is therefore important for the data creator to evaluate whether the file in question has reuse value in that particular format. In addition to the image itself, many vector image applications allow the inclusion of scripts (e.g. JavaScript, AppleScript or VBScript) within files. If such scripts are seen as being worth preserving then they should be stored and documented separately to the image.

Important Aspects of Vector Images for Preservation:

Significant properties of a vector image revolve around the geometry of the image, the vector objects and their relationships, and the conventions (colors, line types and weights) used within the file, as well as maintaining the appearance of these throughout file migrations and archiving. The following elements are those that should be monitored during the archiving of vector files:

- Points, paths (open or closed) and objects (e.g. text, referenced or embedded objects).
- Basic shapes/Primitives (e.g. rectangle, circle, ellipse, etc.).
- Image structure (i.e. the grouping and layering of objects).
- Textual elements.
- Clipping and masking.
- Transformations and Coordinate Systems (if present, though these are mostly present in GIS and CAD vector files).

In addition to ensuring that these specific vector elements remain physically present within a file in the same format, there are a number of obvious properties that can be applied to these. Where standardized conventions exist and have been followed (such as specific meanings associated with certain line colors or dash types), it is essential that these properties and formatting be maintained in archived files. Such properties include:

- Line width, cap and join types.
- Miter limit.
- Dash pattern and offset.
- Color.
- Opacity.
- Rendering.
- Interior definition.
- Gradient and gradient smoothness.
- Pattern.
- Text attributes such as font size, weight or style.

General Checks

When migrating a file to a new format, aside from the obvious visible elements, it is also important to check for hidden information such as invisible objects or layers and to assess the relevance or suitability of these for archiving. Linked data, such as embedded raster files or external fonts, may also be present in the original image and the appearance of such data should be maintained through any file migration. Successfully preserving a vector file is largely dependent on the nature of the original, its complexity and whether it contains pure vector data or incorporates raster data as well. Such mixed files may require the separation of data types into suitable preservation formats.

Additional Metadata for Vector Images

Metadata for vector images is discussed in detail in *The Significant Properties of Vector Images* (Coyne et al. 2007), from which the elements below are taken, and on the JISC Digital Media page discussing Metadata and Digital Images (JISC Digital Media 2012c). The elements below (Tables 3.16 and 3.17) are largely Dublin Core elements that are most usefully generated by the image creator. In addition, some technical elements are suggested (only a subset of those presented in *The Significant Properties of Vector Images*), which may be optionally completed by the data creator.

Table 3.16: General metadata for vector images

Element	Description
Identifier	A unique identifier for the image, usually the filename.
Title/Caption	The title of the image or a suitable caption.
Description/Purpose	Description of the image.
Creator	Name of image creator.
Date	Creation date.
Rights	Details of copyright or other rights and holder details.
Keywords	Keywords e.g. period, site or feature terms. Use suitable thesauri where they exist.
Provenance/Relationship to Other Documents	Description of where the image originated and how (if relevant) it is related to other files.
Conventions	If applicable and not contained within the document, an explanation of all conventions used (colors, layers, line styles, line weights, etc.).

Table 3.17: Technical metadata for vector images

Element	Description
File Format and Version	e.g. SVG 1.1
File Size	Size of the file in bytes
Software	Software used to create the image e.g. Adobe Illustrator

Vector images should be structured logically and in a manner that suits the particular project. A file structure may reflect a specific site or feature or separate instances of fieldwork or photographic survey. Where metadata is to be preserved, it is suggested that it be extracted and stored in a simple text (plain or delimited) or XML structure in a 'documentation' folder alongside the preserved images.

3.4.8 Common File Formats for Vector Images

How to use this table:

Table 3.18 below describes common file formats for vector images as well as their archival equivalents. Each format includes the following:

- File Extension.
- Whether the format is considered 'archival'.
- If the format is not 'archival' what format it should be converted to for archiving.
- Program or Standard associated with the file.
- Notes on the format.

Table 3.18: Common file formats for vector images

Extension	Notes
.PDF/A	✔ **This is an archival format** See full description under Documents and Texts, section 3.2.3. SVG may be preferable to PDF/A for vector images as it captures higher levels of detail and is reusable.
.SVG	✔ **This is an archival format** An open, XML-based standard used to describe 2-D vector graphics and developed by the W3C. In many cases SVG is used on the web together with JavaScript to provide certain functionality. In such cases the container (i.e. the web page) and SVG must be treated as linked files and both preserved and/or presented together.

Extension	Notes
.AI	**This is a commonly used, but not archival format. Check with your repository on whether it is accepted or needs conversion prior to submission. SVG or PDF/A should be used instead.** A proprietary, primarily 2-D, layer-based raster/vector format used by Adobe Illustrator. The format itself has changed throughout its history with early versions being based on PostScript. 3-D capabilities were introduced with Illustrator CS. Although popular and a market leader, the file format is not well supported by other applications and is therefore not suitable for preservation.
.CDR	**This is NOT an archival format. SVG or PDF/A should be used instead.** A proprietary layer-based 2-D format used by CorelDRAW. Similar to the Illustrator AI file format, CDR can hold both raster and vector data but is not well supported by other applications. Not suitable for preservation.
.EPS .EPSF .EPSI	**This is NOT an archival format. SVG or PDF/A should be used instead.** Essentially EPS is a restricted, self-contained Postscript file that can be embedded into another document. EPS may contain vector or bitmap data and fonts and a preview image are normally also included. EPS headers often contain a version number and some programs may reject a file if the version number is absent. As with Postscript, EPS is considered not suitable for preservation due to the availability of more appropriate formats.
.PDF	**This is a commonly used, but not archival format. Check with your repository on whether it is accepted or needs conversion prior to submission. *SVG or PDF/A should be used instead.*** PDF is a subset of Postscript developed by Adobe. Limited to purely page description, PDF incorporates a number of specialized subsets designed for specific purposes (e.g. archiving or engineering). The PDF format is designed primarily for platform-independent document sharing. PDF content can be ASCII text in some cases but the files are more commonly compressed and are therefore binary. PDF/A profile files are considered suitable for preservation but, due to the restrictions required to make them largely self-contained, may not be suitable for all types of content.
.PS	**This is NOT an archival format. SVG or PDF/A should be used instead.** Postscript is a programming language developed by Adobe to describe the appearance of text and images in a device-independent manner. The format has a number of derivatives, notably EPS and PDF, the latter having slowly supplanted Postscript in terms of popularity. Although potentially suitable for preservation, Postscript is no longer commonly used and newer alternatives such as PDF/A present a more robust preservation format.

Extension	Notes
.SWF .FLA .SWD .FLV .SWC .SWT	**This is NOT an archival format. SVG or PDF/A should be used instead.** Flash is a 2-D vector-based animation format optimized for web delivery. The format specifications are freely available but certain elements are still believed to be closed. Flash files are not limited purely to vector images but incorporate scripting and other multimedia to provide a range of functionality.
.WMF .EMF	**This is NOT an archival format. SVG or PDF/A should be used instead.** A proprietary vector-based file format that uses Graphics Device Interface (GDI) commands to render an image. EMF is an enhanced version of the WMF standard for 32-bit architectures. Not suitable for preservation.
.CGM	**This is NOT an archival format. SVG or PDF/A should be used instead.** A 2-D raster/vector format of some vintage and a documented standard format (ISO/IEC 8632). A subset of the format, WebCGM, has been developed over recent years by the W3C as a version of the format suitable for use of the web (W3C 2010). As an open documented standard, WebCGM has potential as a preservation format but is largely superseded by SVG.

3.5 OTHER FORMATS

To this point, we have provided an overview about digitally archiving file types commonly used for archaeological projects. Basic and general file types for documents and texts, databases and spreadsheets, and images have been described.

In addition to the files discussed here, there are a wide variety of other formats used within archaeology that data creators should be aware of and these are covered in detail in the online *Guides to Good Practice*.

Audio and Video

Audio and video files are increasingly being created as common components of archaeological projects either to record the archaeological process itself or as a means of displaying and disseminating data (e.g. 'fly through' video of 3-D data).

Survey and Sensory Data

Data resulting from a wide variety of survey types is a frequent component of many archaeological projects. Such data types are covered under the section 'Data Collection and Fieldwork' in the online *Guides to Good Practice* and include techniques such as:

- Aerial Survey.
- Geophysics.
- Marine Survey.
- Laser Scanning.
- Close-Range Photogrammetry.

Data Analysis and Visualization

In addition to the vector (image) data discussed here, common vector data formats associated with CAD and GIS applications such as DXF, DWG and SHP formats are frequent components of archaeological projects and are dealt with in the online *Guides to Good Practice* in separate chapters focused on CAD and GIS data.

ARCHAEOLOGY DATA SERVICE (ADS)

The Archaeology Data Service archives, disseminates and catalogues high-quality digital resources of long-term interest to archaeologists. Its geographical remit is to provide digital archiving facilities for all areas of the world in which UK archaeologists have research interests. The ADS collections scope is thus international. Archaeologists who are creating fieldwork and excavation digital archives are invited to consider archiving these resources with the ADS.

ADS staff are available to consult with potential depositors by email or telephone during office hours (9–5, Monday to Friday).

Collections Policy

http://archaeologydataservice.ac.uk/advice/collectionsPolicy

The ADS Collections Policy document covers four main areas:

- Collections Development – focuses on the scope and nature of the content collected by the ADS.
- Collections Management – provides a framework for the administration, description and storage of digital data.
- Preservation – defines long-term strategies for the archiving of collections.
- Access and Use – specifies where and how the ADS collections may be used, and identifies primary users.

The Collections Policy document should also be read in conjunction with the ADS Sensitive Data Policy (http://archaeologydataservice.ac.uk/advice/sensitiveDataPolicy).

ADS Charging Policy

http://archaeologydataservice.ac.uk/advice/chargingPolicy

The ADS Charging Policy applies charging levels based on four elements of work: Management and Administration; Ingest; Dissemination; and Storage and Refreshment. Emphasis on any of these four elements may differ according the nature of the project. In addition day rates may vary.

Deposit Formats

http://archaeologydataservice.ac.uk/advice/guidelinesForDepositors

Although the information in this Guide has acted as the basis for ADS ingest and archiving processes, specific delivery formats and metadata are required by the ADS and are outlined in the ADS Guidelines for Depositors where they are regularly reviewed.

Rights Management

http://archaeologydataservice.ac.uk/advice/termsOfUseAndAccess

Although outlined in the Collections Policy, the ADS Copyright and Liability Statement and Common Access Agreement are also directly available within the Terms of Use and Access to ADS resources.

DIGITAL ANTIQUITY

Digital Antiquity supports access to and preservation of archaeological information through its digital repository tDAR (The Digital Archaeological Record). While based in the United States, tDAR's scope is international and accepts archaeological materials from all seven continents.

Digital Antiquity staff are available for consultation during normal business hours. Digital Antiquity will accept a wide range of digital archaeological data for the tDAR repository. Data and documents contributed to the tDAR repository may include digital files related to a wide range of archaeological investigations and topics, e.g., archives and collections, field studies of various scales and intensities, and historical, methodological, synthetic, or theoretical studies.

Pricing

Please see the tDAR website (http://www.tdar.org) for up-to-date information on pricing. In general, tDAR pricing is based on the size (both file size and number of files) as well as complexity of the item. Large and complex projects may benefit from a more direct consultation; please contact Digital Antiquity.

Terms of Use

Knowledge gained through the efforts of many researchers is shared through tDAR in order to encourage and facilitate archaeological and related research. Use of this information is subject only to the minimal conditions of a Creative Commons Attribution license (as adapted) but applicable whether or not the data provided by this site are legally subject to copyright.

Users of tDAR may copy or distribute its content or to use it in derivative works (e.g., to publish or otherwise distribute an argument based on analyses of these data) under the following four conditions:

1. All uses and applications of tDAR content must be accompanied by proper citation and attribution of relevant contributors (as provided by tDAR with the content).
2. For any redistribution of information resources, must clearly cite and attribute relevant contributors, and make clear to others the license terms of this work.
3. Users agree that they will not use content obtained through tDAR in ways that could be reasonably expected to lead, directly or indirectly, to damage to the archaeological record.

4. Users must acknowledge that neither the Center for Digital Antiquity, its sponsors and associates, nor those individuals and institutions providing content through tDAR, guarantee the accuracy or usability of the content and further agree that they may not hold any of these parties liable for any direct or consequential damage arising from their use of tDAR or its content.

Deposit Formats

Digital Antiquity accepts in tDAR many of the formats and file-types described throughout the guides, and is constantly working to add support for additional formats as is technically feasible. Like many digital repositories, tDAR accepts not only archival formats, but industry standard and commonly used formats as well. Please see the tDAR website for an up-to-date list.

Bibliography

Note: All bibliographic links were verified live as of 10th January 2013.

ACHP (Advisory Council on Historic Preservation) (2008) ACHP Policy Statement: Archaeology, Heritage Tourism, and Education. Advisory Council on Historic Preservation, Washington, DC. Accessed at http://www.achp.gov/ArchPolicy.pdf

Aitchison, K. (2010) 'United Kingdom archaeology in economic crisis'. In K. Aitchison and N. Schlanger (eds) *Archaeology and the Global Economic Crisis: Multiple Impacts, Possible Solutions.* Culture Lab Editions. Accessed at http://www.ace-archaeology.eu/fichiers/25Archaeology-and-the-crisis.pdf

Anderson, S., Pringle, M., Eadie, M., Austin, T., Wilson, A. and Polfreman, M. (2006) *Digital Images Archiving Study.* AHDS. Accessed at http://www.jisc.ac.uk/whatwedo/programmes/preservation/imagesarchiving.aspx

Archaeology Data Service (2012a) *Archaeological Records of Europe – Networked Access (ARENA).* Accessed at http://archaeologydataservice.ac.uk/Arena2/

Archaeology Data Service (2012b) *Transatlantic Archaeology Gateway (TAG).* Accessed at http://archaeologydataservice.ac.uk/TAG/

Archaeology Data Service (2012c) *Guidelines for Depositors.* Accessed at http://archaeologydataservice.ac.uk/advice/guidelinesForDepositors

Arts and Humanities Data Service (AHDS) (2006) Preservation Handbooks. Accessed at http://www.ahds.ac.uk/preservation/ahds-preservation-documents.htm

Arts and Humanities Data Service (2007) *Guides to Good Practice.* Accessed at http://www.ahds.ac.uk/archaeology/creating/guides/index.htm

Austin, T. and Mitcham, J. (2007) *Preservation and Management Strategies for Exceptionally Large Data Formats: 'Big Data',* Archaeology Data Service. Accessed at http://archaeologydataservice.ac.uk/attach/bigData/bigdata_final_report_1.3.pdf

Bachmann, E. (2010) *Xbase (&dBASE) File Format Description.* Accessed at http://www.clicketyclick.dk/databases/xbase/format/index.html

Beagrie, N. (2006) Lifecycle modelling: the background. Presented at: LIFE Conference, London, UK. Accessed at http://discovery.ucl.ac.uk/1851/

Bentley Historical Library (2009) *PDF/A (ISO 19005-1) FAQs.* Accessed at http://bentley.umich.edu/uarphome/bestprac/pdfafaqs.php

British Library (2012) *Digital Preservation.* Accessed at http://www.bl.uk/aboutus/stratpolprog/digi/digitalpreservation/index.html

Brown, A. (2008a) *Digital Preservation Guidance Note 1: Selecting File Formats for Long-Term Preservation.* The National Archives. Accessed at http://www.nationalarchives.gov.uk/documents/selecting-file-formats.pdf

Brown, A. (2008b) *Digital Preservation Guidance Note 2: Selecting Storage Media for Long-Term Preservation.* The National Archives. Accessed at http://www.nationalarchives.gov.uk/documents/selecting-storage-media.pdf

Brown, A. (2009) *Digital Preservation Guidance Note 5: Image Compression.* The National Archives. Accessed at http://www.nationalarchives.gov.uk/documents/image_compression.pdf

Buckley, R. (2008) *JPEG 2000 – a Practical Digital Preservation Standard?* DPC Technology Watch Series Report 08-01. Digital Preservation Coalition. Accessed at http://www.dpconline.org/component/docman/doc_download/87-jpeg-2000-a-practical-digital-preservation-standard

Buckley, R. (2009) *JPEG2000 as a Preservation and Access Format for the Wellcome Trust Digital Library.* King's Digital Consultancy Services, King's College, London. Accessed at http://wellcomelibrary.blogspot.com/2009/09/wellcome-library-to-use-jpeg2000-image.html

Center for Digital Antiquity (2012) Web sites for the Center for Digital Antiquity and the Digital Archaeological Record. Accessed at http://www.digitalantiquity.org and http://www.tdar.org

Center for Research Libraries (CRL), Research Libraries Group, and National Archives and Records Administration (2007) *Trustworthy Repositories Audit & Certification (TRAC): Criteria and Checklist.* Accessed at http://www.crl.edu/sites/default/files/attachments/pages/trac_0.pdf

Center for Research Libraries (CRL) (2012) Certification and Assessment web page. Accessed at http://www.crl.edu/archiving-preservation/digital-archives/certification-and-assessment-digital-repositories

Childs, S. T., editor (2010) Special Issue: The Dollars and Sense of Managing Archaeological Collections. *Heritage Management* **3**(2): 155–289.

Childs, S. T. and Kagan, S. (2008) *A Decade of Study into Repository Fees for Archeological Collections.* Studies in Archeology Program, National Park Service, Washington, DC. Accessed at http://core.tdar.org/document/377048; doi:10.6067/XCV8NS0T7S

Condron, F., Richards, J., Robinson, D. and Wise, A. (1999) *Strategies for Digital Data – Findings and Recommendations from Digital Data in Archaeology: a Survey of User Needs.* Archaeology Data Service, York.

Consultative Committee for Space Data Systems (2012) *Reference Model for an Open Archival Information System (OAIS).* Accessed at http://public.ccsds.org/publications/archive/650x0m2.pdf

Costen, D., Gevaux, N., Milner, E. and Russell, B. (2012) *Gazetteer of Archaeological Investigation in England.* School of Applied Sciences, Bournemouth University. Accessed at http://csweb.bournemouth.ac.uk/aip/gaz2010/AIP2010All.pdf

Coyne, M., Duce, D., Hopgood, B., Mallen, G. and Stapleton, M. (2007) *The Significant Properties of Vector Images.* JISC. Accessed at http://www.jisc.ac.uk/media/documents/programmes/preservation/vector_images.pdf

Cultural Heritage Partners, PLLC (2012) Legal Analysis of Federal Requirements for Curation of Digital Archaeological Documents and Data. Report prepared for Office of the General Counsel, Arizona State University. Accessed at http://www.digitalantiquity.org/wp-uploads/2011/07/CHPFinal.pdf

Data Seal of Approval (2012) *Quality Guidelines for Digital Research Data.* Accessed at http://datasealofapproval.org/sites/default/files/DSA%20booklet_2-0_engels_mei2010.pdf

Day, M. (2005) 'Metadata', in S. Ross and M. Day (eds) *DCC Digital Curation Manual.* Accessed at http://www.dcc.ac.uk/resources/curation-reference-manual/completed-chapters/metadata

DCMI Usage Board (2012) *DCMI Metadata Terms*. Accessed at http://dublincore.org/documents/2012/06/14/dcmi-terms/

Departmental Consulting Archeologist (2009) *The Secretary of the Interior's Report to Congress on the Federal Archeological Program, 1998–2003*. Archeology Program, National Park Service, Washington, D.C. Accessed at http://core.tdar.org/document/2510; doi:10.6067/XCV81N7ZR4

Departmental Consulting Archeologist (2010) *The Secretary of the Interior's Report to Congress on the Federal Archeological Program, 2004–2007*. Archeology Program, National Park Service, Washington, D.C. Accessed at http://core.tdar.org/document/378315; doi:10.6067/XCV8MS3S4Q

Digital Curation Centre (DCC) (2008) *Data Lifecycle Model*. Accessed at http://www.dcc.ac.uk/resources/curation-lifecycle-model

Digital Preservation Coalition (2012) *Digital Preservation Handbook*. Accessed at http://www.dpconline.org/advice/preservationhandbook

Eadie, M. (2005) *Preservation Handbook: Bitmap (Raster) Images*. AHDS. Accessed at http://www.ahds.ac.uk/preservation/Bitmap-preservation-handbook_d6.pdf

Eiteljorg, H. (2004) 'Computing for archaeologists', in S. Schreibman, R. Siemens and J. Unsworth, *A Companion to Digital Humanities*. Blackwell, London: 20–30.

English Heritage (n.d.) *NMR Monument Type Thesaurus*. Accessed at http://thesaurus.english-heritage.org.uk/thesaurus.asp?thes_no=1

Fanning, B. A. (2008) *Preserving the Data Explosion: Using PDF*. DPC Technology Watch Series Report 08. Accessed at http://www.dpconline.org/docs/reports/dpctw08-02.pdf

Ford, M. (2010) 'Archaeology: hidden treasure', *Nature* 464: 826–27. Accessed at http://www.nature.com/news/2010/100407/full/464826a.html

Fowler, P. (2000a) *Landscape Plotted and Pieced: Landscape History and Local Archaeology in Fyfield and Overton, Wiltshire*. The Society of Antiquaries of London, Oxbow Books.

Fowler, P. (2000b) *Fyfield and Overton Project, 1959–1998*. Archaeology Data Service, York. Accessed at doi:10.5284/1000336

Getty Research Institute (n.d.) *Getty Thesaurus of Geographic Names Online*. Accessed at http://www.getty.edu/research/tools/vocabularies/tgn/

Gillesse, R., Rog, J. andVerheusen, A. (2008) *Alternative File Formats for Storing Master Images of Digitisation Projects*. National Library of the Netherlands. Accessed at http://www.kb.nl/hrd/dd/dd_links_en_publicaties/publicaties/alternative_file_formats_for_storing_masters_2_1.pdf

Higgins, S. (2006) *What are Metadata Standards*. Digital Curation Centre Standards Watch Paper. Accessed at http://www.dcc.ac.uk/resources/briefing-papers/standards-watch-papers/what-are-metadata-standards

Heydegger, V. (2008) 'Analysing the impact of file formats on data integrity', *Archiving* 2008, Volume 5. Accessed at http://www.imaging.org/IST/store/epub.cfm?abstrid=38884

Internet Archaeology (2012) *The LEAP Projects*. Accessed at http://intarch.ac.uk/leap/index.html

JISC Digital Media (2012a) *Case Study: Learning Lessons from Other Digitisation Projects*. Accessed at http://www.jiscdigitalmedia.ac.uk/casestudy/learning-lessons-from-other-digitisation-projects

JISC Digital Media (2012b) *Copyright and Other Rights for Creating Time-based Media Resources*. Accessed at http://www.jiscdigitalmedia.ac.uk/crossmedia/advice/copyright-and-other-rights-for-creating-time-based-media-resources/

JISC Digital Media (2012c) *Metadata and Digital Images*. Accessed at http://www.jiscdigitalmedia.ac.uk/stillimages/advice/metadata-and-digital-images/

JISC Digital Media (2012d) *Introduction to the Vector Image Format*. Accessed at http://www.jiscdigitalmedia.ac.uk/stillimages/advice/introduction-to-the-vector-image-format

JISC Legal (2007)*e-Repositories and the Law Essentials*. Accessed at http://www.jisclegal.ac.uk/Portals/12/Documents/PDFs/erepessentials.pdf

JISC Legal (2011a) *Copyright Law Essentials*. Accessed at http://www.jisclegal.ac.uk/LegalAreas/CopyrightIPR/CopyrightLawEssentials.aspx

JISC Legal (2011b) *Archived – Intellectual Property Law Essentials.* Accessed at http://www.jisclegal.ac.uk/LegalAreas/CopyrightIPR/IPREssentials.aspx

Joint Photographic Experts Group (JPEG) (2007) *JPEG 2000 Metadata.* Accessed at http://www.jpeg.org/jpeg2000/metadata.html

Kintigh, K. and Altschul, J. (2010) 'Sustaining the digital archaeological record', *Heritage Management* 3(2): 264–74. Accessed at http://core.tdar.org/document/376850; doi:10.6067/XCV87H1HWV

LaBarca, J. E. (2010) 'Image storage and permanence considerations in the long-term preservation of photographic images – update 2010', *Journal of Physics: Conference Series* **231**: 012008. Accessed at http://dx.doi.org/10.1088/1742-6596/231/1/012008

Library of Congress (2011) *Guidelines for Electronic Preservation of Visual Materials.* Accessed at http://www.loc.gov/preservation/resources/rt/guide/guid_dig.html

Library of Congress (2012a) Digital Preservation web site. Accessed at http://www.digitalpreservation.gov/

Library of Congress (2012b) MODS: Metadata Object Description Schema. Accessed at http://www.loc.gov/standards/mods/

Lipe, William D. (1997) *Report on the Second Conference on Renewing Our National Archaeological Program, February 9–11, 1997.* Accessed at http://core.tdar.org/document/378316; doi:10.6067/XCV87M0790

Lowe, D. and Bennett, M.J. (2009) *A Status Report on JPEG 2000 Implementation for Still Images: The UConn Survey.* UConn Libraries Published Works. Paper 19. Accessed at http://digitalcommons.uconn.edu/libr_pubs/19

McManamon, F.P. (2000) *Renewing the National Archaeological Program: Final Report of Accomplishments. A Report to the Board of the Society for American Archaeology from the Task Force Chair.* Society for American Archaeology, Washington, D.C. Accessed at http://core.tdar.org/document/378319; doi:10.6067/XCV8H41QSP

McManamon, F.P. and Kintigh, K. (2010) 'Digital Antiquity: transforming archaeological data into knowledge', *SAA Archaeological Record* **10**(2): 37–40. Accessed at http://core.tdar.org/document/376844; doi:10.6067/XCV8QF8S60

McManamon, F.P., Kintigh, K. and Brin, A. (2010) 'Digital Antiquity and the Digital Archaeological Record (tDAR): Broadening Access and Ensuring Long-Term Preservation for Digital Archaeological Data'. *The CSA Newsletter*, Bryn Mawr, PA. Accessed at http://core.tdar.org/document/376847; doi:10.6067/XCV8KS6QT2

Metadata Working Group (2009) *Guidelines for Handling Image Metadata.* Version 1.0.1 Accessed at http://www.metadataworkinggroup.org/pdf/mwg_guidance.pdf

Michener, W.K., Brunt, J.W., Helly, J.J., Kirchner, T.B. and Stafford, S.G. (1997) 'Nongeospatial Metadata for the Ecological Sciences', *Ecological Applications* **7**(1): 330–42.

Montague, L. (2009) *Significant Properties Testing Report: Raster Images.* InSPECT Project website. Accessed at http://www.significantproperties.org.uk/rasterimages-testingreport.html

National Academies (2009) *Ensuring the Integrity, Accessibility, and Stewardship of Research Data in the Digital Age.* The National Academies Press, Washington, D.C. Accessed at http://www.nap.edu/openbook.php?record_id=12615&page=1

National Archives (2007) *Frequently Asked Questions About Optical Media.* Accessed at http://www.archives.gov/records-mgmt/faqs/optical.html

National Archives (n.d.) *Frequently Asked Questions (FAQs) about Optical Storage Media: Storing Temporary Records on CDs and DVDs.* Accessed at http://www.archives.gov/records-mgmt/initiatives/temp-opmedia-faq.html

National Space Science Data Center (NSSDC) (2012) *Welcome to the National Space Science Data Center, NASA's permanent archive for space science mission data.* Accessed at http://nssdc.gsfc.nasa.gov/

Nature (2009a) 'Editorial: Data's shameful neglect', *Nature* **461** (7261): 145. Accessed at http://www.nature.com/nature/journal/v461/n7261/full/461145a.html

Nature (2009b) 'Opinion: Prepublication data sharing', *Nature* **461** (7261): 168–70. Accessed at http://www.nature.com/nature/journal/v461/n7261/full/461168a.html

Nelson, Bryn (2009) 'Data sharing: empty archives', *Nature* **461** (7261): 160–63. Accessed at http://www.nature.com/news/2009/090909/full/461160a.html

NISO (2004) *Understanding Metadata.* NISO Press. Accessed at http://www.niso.org/standards/resources/UnderstandingMetadata.pdf

Open Government Initiative (2012) The White House, Open Government Initiative web site. Accessed at http://www.whitehouse.gov/open/about/policy

Rothenberg, J. (1999) *Avoiding Technological Quicksand: Finding a Viable Technical Foundation for Digital Preservation.* Accessed at http://www.clir.org/PUBS/reports/rothenberg/pub77.pdf

RLG (2002) *Trusted Digital Repositories: Attributes and Responsibilities. Research Libraries Group.* Accessed at http://www.oclc.org/research/activities/past/rlg/trustedrep/repositories.pdf

Schofield, Paul N., Bubela, T., Weaver, T., Brown, S.D., Hancock, J.M., Einhorn, D., Tocchini-Valentini, G., Hrabe de Angelis, M. and Rosenthal, N. (2009) 'Opinion: post-publication sharing of data and tools;, *Nature* **461** (7261): 171–73. Accessed at http://www.nature.com/nature/journal/v461/n7261/full/461171a.html

Science (2011) 'Dealing with data: special section', *Science* **331** (11 February 2011): 692–728. Accessed at http://www.sciencemag.org/content/331/6018.toc

Swain, H. (1998) *A Survey of Archaeological Archives in England.* English Heritage and Museums & Galleries Commission, London.

Swiss Federal Archives (n.d.) Archiving of Databases: SIARD Suite. Accessed at http://www.bar.admin.ch/dienstleistungen/00823/00825/index.html?lang=en

tDAR (2011) *Data Dictionary.* Accessed at http://dev.tdar.org/confluence/display/TDAR/Data+Dictionary

Terotechnology Handbook (1978) HMSO.

Thompson, M. S., Abbott, D., Breternitz, C. and Hill, R. (2012) *Pueblo Grande (AZ U:9:7 [ASM]): Monitoring, Testing, and Data Recovery Projects.* Accessed at http://core.tdar.org/collection/10927

Todd, M. (2009) *File Formats for Preservation.* DPC Technology Watch Series Report 09-02. Accessed at http://www.dpconline.org/publications/technology-watch-reports

van Ballegooie, M. and Duff, W. (2006) 'Archival metadata', in S. Ross and M. Day (eds) *DCC Digital Curation Manual.* Accessed at http://www.dcc.ac.uk/resources/curation-reference-manual/completed-chapters/archival-metadata

UKOLN (2004) *Good Practice Guide for Developers of Cultural Heritage Web Services.* Accessed at http://www.ukoln.ac.uk/interop-focus/gpg

UK Data Archive (2012) *Documentation & Metadata Overview.* Accessed at http://www.data-archive.ac.uk/create-manage/document/overview

US Copyright Office (2009) *Fair Use.* Factsheet FL102. Accessed at http://www.copyright.gov/fls/fl102.html

W3C (2010) *WebCGM 2.1.* Accessed at http://www.w3.org/TR/2010/REC-webcgm21-20100301/

Watts, J. (2011) *Policies, Preservation, and Access to Digital Resources: The Digital Antiquity 2010 National Repositories Survey.* Publications in Digital Antiquity No. 2. Accessed at http://core.tdar.org/document/378318; doi:10.6067/XCV8CC1022

Wynne, M. and Yeates, S. (2005) *Preservation Handbook: Plain Text.* AHDS Preservation Handbook. Accessed at http://ota.ahds.ac.uk/documents/preservation/preservation_plaintext.pdf